Uncovering
STUDENT THINKING
in
MATHEMATICS

Uncovering
STUDENT THINKING
in
MATHEMATICS

25

Formative
Assessment
Probes

CHERYL M. ROSE   LESLIE MINTON   CAROLYN ARLINE

Foreword by ANNE DAVIES

CORWIN PRESS
A SAGE Publications Company
Thousand Oaks, CA 91320

For information:

 Corwin Press
A Sage Publications Company
2455 Teller Road
Thousand Oaks, California 91320
www.corwinpress.com

Sage Publications Ltd.
1 Oliver's Yard
55 City Road
London EC1Y 1SP
United Kingdom

Sage Publications India Pvt. Ltd.
B-42, Panchsheel Enclave
Post Box 4109
New Delhi 110–017 India

Printed in the United States of America

Library of Congress Cataloging-in-Publication Data
Rose, Cheryl M.
Uncovering student thinking in mathematics : 25 formative assessment probes / Cheryl M. Rose, Leslie Minton, and Carolyn Arline.
      p. cm.
Includes bibliographical references and index.
ISBN 1-4129-4036-2 or 978-1-4129-4036-8 (cloth)
ISBN 1-4129-4037-0 or 978-1-4129-4037-5 (pbk.)
   1. Mathematical ability—Testing. 2. Mathematics—Study and teaching—Evaluation.
 I. Minton, Leslie.
II. Arline, Carolyn. III.
Title.

QA11.2.R67 2007
372.7—dc22   2006022366

This book is printed on acid-free paper.

        07   08   09   10   10   9   8   7   6   5   4   3   2

Acquisitions Editor: Rachel Livsey
Editorial Assistant: Phyllis Cappello
Production Editor: Libby Larson
Copy Editor: Jackie Tasch
Typesetter: C&M Digitals (P) Ltd.
Proofreader: Jennifer Ang
Indexer: Sheila Bodell
Cover Designer: Monique Hahn
Graphic Designer: Karine Hovsepian

Contents

Foreword

"Change starts when someone sees the next step."

William Drayton

We know students learn more when we begin with the end—the learning destination—in mind. It is also true students learn more when we begin with them—finding out what they know and what they need to learn and then using assessment for learning to help them learn more. Watching and listening to learners—assessment that not only informs teaching but also promotes learning—is the foundation of all good teaching.

When adults listen and watch children, take delight in their uniqueness, and believe in the power of their gifts, we act as mirrors giving them some of the courage and faith they will need to live their lives well. As an adult, I loved going home to visit my mom. She would make my favorite foods; we would talk, drink tea, eat treats, and not share with my six siblings. I would bask in her love and pride. Being with her meant seeing me—the best parts of who I was and who I wanted to be—reflected in her eyes.

Like us, students are who they are and what they've experienced. They are like mirrors reflecting what they've seen, heard, done, or had done to them. Sometimes it is hard for us to look or listen. It takes courage on our part to listen beyond the baggy jeans, grubby T-shirts, dirty faces, and attitudes to see children as they are and as they might be. When we listen to children, watch them learn, and respond thoughtfully, we have a chance to see them in ways no one else might and they have a chance to see themselves that way.

We work on behalf of children. In these times it can be hard to remember that. Our job is to help them become all they can be. Just as my mom's belief in me continues to give me the courage and faith I need to keep trying, our belief in our students gives them courage and faith so they are more likely to take the risks to learn. The authors of this book show us ways to listen and observe children and their mathematical understandings so we can find better ways to help each child take his or her next learning steps. This book is a gift to educators who "seek to understand before being understood."

—*Anne Davies*

Preface

Mathematics Questions to Uncover and Explore Student Thinking

Overview

With mandates from the No Child Left Behind Act and other state-driven assessment initiatives, substantial amounts of educator time and energy are being spent on developing, implementing, scoring, and analyzing summative assessments of students' mathematical knowledge. Although the importance of summative assessment is recognized, findings point to *formative* assessment as an important strategy in improving student achievement in mathematics.

Formative assessment informs instruction. It takes many forms, the purpose of which is determining students' prior knowledge of a learning target and using that information to drive instruction, moving each student toward understanding of the targeted concepts and procedures. Questioning, observation, and student self-assessment are examples of instructional strategies that educators can incorporate to gain insight into student understanding. These instructional strategies become formative assessment if the results are used to plan and implement learning activities designed to address the specific needs of the students.

This resource focuses on using diagnostic questions, called Mathematics Assessment Probes, to elicit prior understandings and commonly held misconceptions. This elicitation allows the educator to make sound instructional choices based on the specific needs of a particular group of students.

Diagnostic assessment is as important to teaching as a physical exam is to prescribing an appropriate medical regimen. At the outset of any unit of study, certain students are likely to have already mastered some of the skills that the teacher is about to introduce, and others may already understand key concepts. Some students are likely to be deficient in prerequisite skills or harbor misconceptions. Armed with this diagnostic information, a teacher gains greater insight into what to teach. (McTighe & O'Connor, 2005, p. 14)

The Mathematics Assessment Probes provided in this resource are tools teachers can use to gather these important insights.

Audience

The collection of Mathematics Assessment Probes and the accompanying Teachers' Notes are designed for the busy K–12 classroom teacher who understands that a growing body of research discusses students' learning difficulties and that thoughtful use of this research in developing and selecting diagnostic assessments promises to enhance the efficiency and effectiveness of mathematics instruction.

Background

The probes are designed to uncover student understandings and misunderstandings based on research findings, and they have been pilot-tested and field-tested with teachers and students.

Because the probes are based on cognitive research, examples exist in multiple resources, but no previous publication had collected them and designed them for the specific purpose of action research in the classroom. In the actual research reports, the questions used in these mathematics assessment probes are spread throughout the material and are not ready for classroom use. In this book, the probes were developed using the process described in *Mathematics Curriculum Topic Study: Bridging the Gap Between Standards and Practice* (Keeley & Rose, 2006). They were originally piloted with the Maine, New Hampshire, and Vermont teachers participating in the National Science Foundation (NSF)-funded Northern New England Co-Mentoring Network. The use of the probes was expanded to include teacher leaders and mathematics specialists who are Fellows in the Maine Governor's Academy for Mathematics and Science Education Leadership, a State Mathematics and Science Partnership Project: Mathematics: Access and Teaching in High School (MATHS), and various other mathematics professional development programs offered through the Maine Mathematics and Science Alliance.

Organization

This book is organized to provide readers with the purpose, structure, and development of the Mathematics Assessment Probes, as well as to support the use of applicable research and instructional strategies in mathematics classrooms.

Chapter 1 provides in-depth information about the process and design of the mathematics probes along with the development of the QUEST cycle. Chapter 2 highlights instructional implications and images from practice to illuminate how easily the probes can be used in mathematics classrooms and how many ways they can be employed. Chapters 3 to 5 are the collections of probes categorized by content strands, within grade spans, with accompanying Teachers' Notes that provide the specific research and instructional strategies designed to speak directly to the mathematics involved specific to the probe.

Acknowledgments

We would like to thank Page Keeley, our science colleague, who designed the process for developing diagnostic assessment probes. Without her, this book would not have been possible.

We would like to thank the Northern New England Co-Mentoring Network (NNECN) mentors and mentees, the Mathematics: Access and Teaching in High School (MATHS) teachers, and the School Administrative District No. 11 elementary educators for their ongoing support, continued feedback, student work, and valuable conversations.

We would like to give special thanks to the following individuals for their willingness to open their classroom(s) and to their students for their willingness to share so much of their great mathematics thinking: JanWillem Musters, Christine Downing, and Connie Upshultz.

We would like to acknowledge the contributions of the following educators who supplied student work and feedback for this project: Rich Clonan, Lauren Dokas, Joelle Drake, Elizabeth Hall, Nancy Gorden, Judy Parent, Gloria Powers, Sue Saucier, Angela Smith, Mary Sanborn, Mary Ann Kotros, Anne Marriner, and Sue Williamson.

In addition, several of our colleagues contributed to this work in many ways, including giving support, examining the probes, and reviewing the manuscript. Thank you to Francis Eberle, Jill Rosenblum, Lynn Farrin, Cynthia Hillman-Forbush, and Debra McIntyre.

The contributions of the following reviewers are gratefully acknowledged:

Richard H. Audet
Associate Professor of Science Education
Roger Williams University
Bristol, RI

Randy Cook
Chemistry/Physics Instructor
Tri County High School
Howard City, MI

About the Authors

 **Cheryl Rose** is the senior program director for mathematics at the Maine Mathematics and Science Alliance (MMSA). Her work at the MMSA is primarily in the areas of leadership, mathematics professional development, and school reform. She is currently the co-principal investigator of the mathematics section of the National Science Foundation (NSF) funded project, Curriculum Topic Study, and principal investigator and project director of a Title IIa State Mathematics and Science Partnership Project, Mathematics: Access and Teaching in High School (MATHS). Prior to working on these projects, Cheryl was the co-principal investigator and project director for MMSA's NSF-funded Local Systemic Change Initiative, Broadening Educational Access to Mathematics in Maine (BEAMM) and she was a fellow in Cohort 4 of the National Academy for Science and Mathematics Education Leadership. Before coming to the MMSA in 2001, Cheryl was a high school and middle school mathematics educator for 10 years. Cheryl received her BS in secondary mathematics education from the University of Maine at Farmington and her MEd in curriculum and instruction from City University in Seattle.

 **Leslie Minton** is currently a mathematics project director for the MMSA, Augusta, Maine. She is currently a co-director of the Teacher Student Learning Continuum, a project funded in part by an award from the Maine Department of Education, which provides financial and technical assistance to five Maine school districts. She is the project director for the Early Mathematical Thinking (EMT) project, a collaboration among 30 Maine school sites engaging in pilot-testing both a professional development course and program assessment materials about the mathematical development of K–4 students. She is a fellow of the second cohort group of the Governor's Academy for Science and Mathematics Educators. She has taught regular and special education for Grades 4 through 12. Leslie received her BS in elementary and special education from the University of Maine at Farmington and her MEd in curriculum, instruction, and assessment from Walden University.

 **Carolyn Arline** is a mathematics specialist for the MMSA and works primarily in the areas of mathematics professional development, leadership, school reform, and assessment. She is currently working on a Title IIa State Mathematics and Science Partnership Project, MATHS, a systematic reform project focusing on improving mathematics teaching and learning in Grades 6 through 12 for nine districts. Carolyn also teaches the Dynamic Classroom Assessment course to Grades 6–12 mathematics teachers. She is a fellow of the second cohort group of the Governor's Academy for Science and Mathematics Educators and was a mathematics mentor in the NSF-funded Northern New England Co-Mentoring Network. Prior to coming to the MMSA in 2004, Carolyn taught high school mathematics and served as a mathematics department chair. She received her BS in secondary mathematics education from the University of Maine at Orono.

Mathematics Assessment Probes

To differentiate instruction effectively, teachers need diagnostic assessment strategies to gauge their students' prior knowledge and uncover their misunderstandings. By accurately identifying and addressing misunderstandings, teachers prevent their students from becoming frustrated and disenchanted with mathematics, which can reinforce the student preconception that "some people don't have the ability to do math." Diagnostic strategies also allow for instruction that builds on individual students' existing understandings while addressing their identified difficulties. The Mathematics Assessment Probes in this book allow teachers to target specific areas of difficulty as identified in research on student learning. Targeting specific areas of difficulty—for example, the transition from reasoning about whole numbers to understanding numbers that are expressed in relationship to other numbers (decimals and fractions)—focuses diagnostic assessment effectively (National Research Council, 2005, p. 310).

Mathematics Assessment Probes represent one approach to diagnostic assessment. They typically include a prompt or question and a series of responses. The probes specifically elicit prior understandings and commonly held misconceptions that may or may not have been uncovered during an instructional unit. This elicitation allows teachers to make instructional choices based on the specific needs of students. Examples of commonly held misconceptions elicited by a Mathematics Assessment Probe include ideas such as *multiplication makes bigger* and *the larger the denominator, the larger the fraction.*

It is important to make the distinction between what we might call a silly mistake and a more fundamental one, which may be the product of a deep-rooted misunderstanding. It is not uncommon for different students to display the same misunderstanding every year. Being aware of and eliciting common misunderstandings and drawing students' attention to them can be a valuable teaching technique (Griffin & Madgwick, 2005).

The process of diagnosing student understandings and misunderstandings and making instructional decisions based on that information is the key to increasing students' mathematical knowledge. To use the Mathematics Assessment Probes for this purpose, teachers need to:

- Determine a question
- Use a probe to examine student understandings and misunderstandings
- Use links to cognitive research to drive next steps in instruction
- Implement the instructional unit or activity
- Determine the impact on learning by asking an additional question

The above process is described in detail in this chapter. The Teachers' Notes that accompany each of the Mathematics Assessment Probes in Chapters 3 through 5 include information on research findings and instructional implications relevant to the individual probe.

WHAT TYPES OF UNDERSTANDINGS AND MISUNDERSTANDINGS DOES A MATHEMATICS ASSESSMENT PROBE UNCOVER?

Developing understanding in mathematics is an important but difficult goal. Being aware of student difficulties and the sources of the difficulties, and designing instruction to diminish them, are important steps in achieving this goal. (Yetkin, 2003)

The Mathematics Assessment Probes are designed to uncover student understandings and misunderstandings; the results are used to inform instruction rather than make evaluative decisions. As shown in Figure 1.1, the understandings include both *conceptual* and *procedural knowledge* and misunderstandings are classified as *common errors* or *overgeneralizations*. Each of these is described in more detail below.

Understandings: Conceptual and Procedural Knowledge

Research has solidly established the importance of conceptual understanding in becoming proficient in a subject. When students understand mathematics, they are able to use their knowledge flexibly. They combine factual knowledge, procedural facility, and conceptual understanding in powerful ways (National Council of Teachers of Mathematics [NCTM], 2000).

Conceptual Understanding

Students demonstrate conceptual understanding in mathematics when they:

- Recognize, label, and generate examples and nonexamples of concepts
- Use and interrelate models, diagrams, manipulatives, and so on
- Know and apply facts and definitions
- Compare, contrast, and integrate concepts and principles
- Recognize, interpret, and apply signs, symbols, and terms
- Interpret assumptions and relationships in mathematical settings

Figure 1.1   Mathematics Assessment Probes

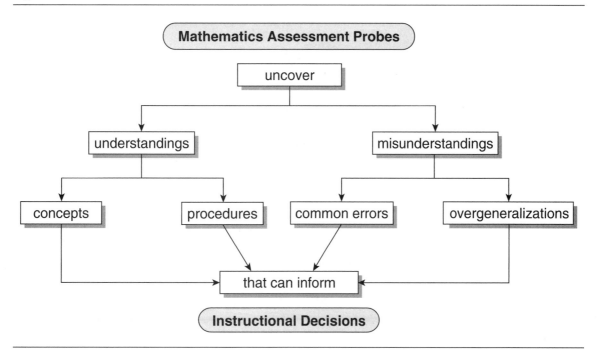

Procedural Knowledge

Students demonstrate procedural knowledge in mathematics when they:

- Select and apply appropriate procedures
- Verify or justify a procedure using concrete models or symbolic methods
- Extend or modify procedures to deal with factors in problem settings
- Use numerical algorithms
- Read and produce graphs and tables
- Execute geometric constructions
- Perform noncomputational skills such as rounding and ordering (U.S. Department of Education, 2003, Chapter 4)

The relationship between understanding concepts and being proficient with procedures is complex. The following description gives an example of how the Mathematics Assessment Probes elicit conceptual or procedural understanding.

The Volume of the Box probe (see Figure 1.2) is designed to elicit whether students understand the formula numerically and quantitatively (NCTM, 2003, p. 101). Students who correctly determine the volume of the first problem, yet choose *C. Not enough information* for the second problem may be able to apply the volume formula, $V = lwh$, when given a length, width, and height but lack the ability to apply the formula to a varied representation of the concept. The following student responses to "Explain Your Reasoning" are indicative of conceptual understanding of the formula:

- "Volume is the area of the base times the height. If you flip this box, the 24 is the base and 4 is the height so $24 \text{ cm}^2 \times 4 \text{ cm}$ is 96 cm^3."

Figure 1.2 Volume of a Box Probe

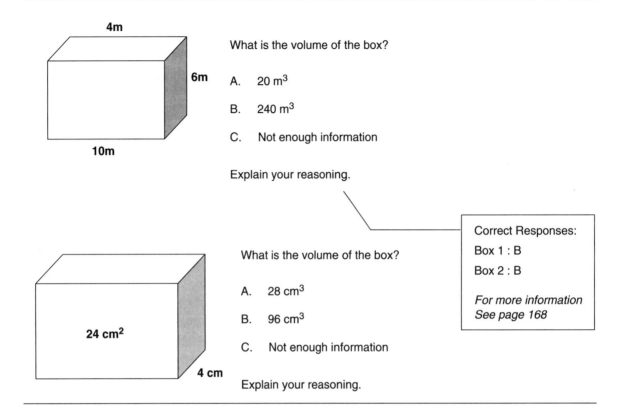

• "You already have some of the information needed. If you rearrange $l \times w \times h$ to fit the information given, you would have $(l \times h) \times w$. You are given that $l \times h$ is 24 cm² and $(24 \text{ cm}^2)\,(4 \text{ cm}) = 96 \text{ cm}^3$."

Misunderstandings: Common Errors and Overgeneralizations

In "Hispanic and Anglo Students' Misconceptions in Mathematics," Jose Mestre summarizes cognitive research as follows:

> Students do not come to the classroom as "blank slates" (Resnick, 1983). Instead, they come with theories constructed from their everyday experiences. They have actively constructed these theories, an activity crucial to all successful learning. Some of the theories that students use to make sense of the world are, however, incomplete half-truths (Mestre, 1987). They are misconceptions.
>
> Misconceptions are a problem for two reasons. First, they interfere with learning when students use them to interpret new experiences. Second, students are emotionally and intellectually attached to their misconceptions because they have actively constructed them. Hence, students give up their misconceptions, which can have such a harmful effect on learning, only with great reluctance.

For the purposes of this book, these misunderstandings or misconceptions will be categorized into *common errors* and *overgeneralizations*. Each of these categories of misunderstandings is described in more detail.

Common Error Patterns

Common error patterns refer to systematic uses of inaccurate/inefficient procedures or strategies. Typically, this type of error pattern indicates non-understanding of an important math concept (University of Kansas, 2005). Examples of common error patterns include consistent misuse of a tool or steps of an algorithm, such as an inaccurate procedure for computing or the misreading of a measurement device. The following description gives an example of how the Mathematics Assessment Probes elicit common error patterns.

The How Long Is the Pencil? probe (see Figure 1.3) is designed to elicit understanding of zero-point. "A significant minority of older children (e.g., fifth grade) respond to nonzero origins by simply reading off whatever number on a ruler aligns with the end of the object (Lehrer et al., 1998a)" (NCTM, 2003, p. 183).

The correct answer is Yes, A and B are of equal length. The measurement for both pencils is 5 inches. Pencil A aligns the tip of the pencil with the end of the ruler, which is not the starting point for accurate measuring. Pencil B aligns the tip of the pencil with the 0 point on the ruler and the eraser ending at the

Figure 1.3 Common Error Probe

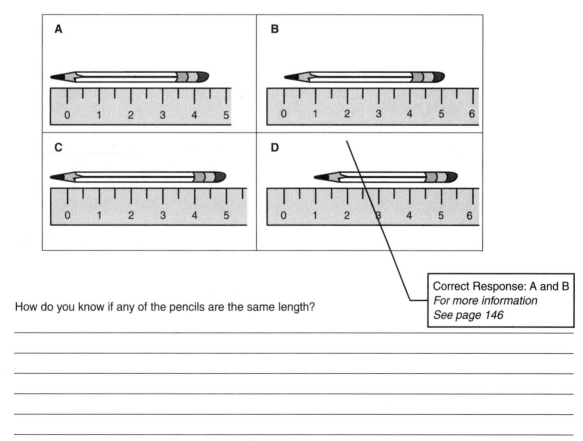

How Long Is the Pencil?

Are any of the pencils the same length?

How do you know if any of the pencils are the same length?

Correct Response: A and B
*For more information
See page 146*

5-inch mark. To reconcile the measurements, students must adjust Pencil A to begin at the 0 point, so that the eraser ends at the 5-inch mark.

Students who choose B and C most likely looked at the eraser of the pencil and judged that they both measured 5 inches. Their error is not considering the beginning point on the ruler as it relates to the beginning of the object being measured. Students who choose A and D most likely considered the inch difference in D but failed to recognize that choice A did not begin at zero, thus making the pencils not an equal length.

Overgeneralizations

Often, students learn an algorithm, rule, or shortcut and then extend this information to another context in an inappropriate way. These misunderstandings are often overgeneralizations from cases that students have seen in prior instruction (Griffin & Madgwick, 2005). To teach in a way that avoids creating any misconceptions is not possible, and we have to accept that students will make some incorrect generalizations that will remain hidden unless the teacher makes specific efforts to uncover them (Askew & Wiliam, 1995).

The following descriptions give two examples of how the Mathematics Assessment Probes elicit overgeneralizations. The Which Is Bigger? multiplication probe (see Figure 1.4) is designed to elicit the overgeneralization of the effect of multiplication, "multiplication always makes bigger," which stems from prior experience with whole numbers. Such overgeneralizations profoundly affect a student's ability to use estimation and check reasonableness of results.

The probe is designed to assess a student's ability to judge the effect of operations when computing with a whole number and a number between 0 and 1. In the field test of this probe, very few students were able to determine the correct answer.

Another type of overgeneralization is uncovered in the Are You Positive? probe (see Figure 1.5). In this example, many students extend the "two negatives make a positive" rule beyond the operation of multiplication.

In addition to uncovering common misunderstandings, the Mathematics Assessment Probes also elicit *uncommon* misconceptions that may not be uncovered and could continue to cause difficulty in understanding a targeted concept. An example of this is highlighted in the following Image From Practice.

Figure 1.4   Which Is Bigger? Probe

Use mental math and estimation to determine which problem results in the greatest answer.

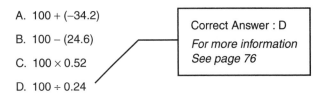

A. 100 + (−34.2)

B. 100 − (24.6)

C. 100 × 0.52

D. 100 ÷ 0.24

Correct Answer : D

*For more information
See page 76*

Please explain your reasoning

Figure 1.5   Are You Positive? Probe

Using mental math, indicate which problems result in a POSITIVE answer.

A. $-(-53 + 92)$

B. $-34 - 27$

C. $93 - (-56)$

D. $(-24)(35)$

E. $(-34)(-54)$

F. $-34 + -56$

G. $\dfrac{-5}{-2}$

H. $\dfrac{-5 - 10}{-(-2)}$

Describe the process that you used to decide whether the problem resulted in a positive answer.

Correct Selections: CEG
For more information
See page 77

Image From Practice: Are They Equal?

In looking over my third-grade students' responses to the Are They Equal? probe (see Figure 1.6), one particular student's thinking captured my attention. I could see she had done the computation correctly, yet she made conclusions about equality that were puzzling. She summarized that equality was decided by the digit in the one's place, which indicated whether the answer was odd or even. Her justification was that "even numbers are equal and odd numbers are not equal." If I had not given this probe, this overgeneralization may not have surfaced.

HOW WERE THE MATHEMATICS ASSESSMENT PROBES DEVELOPED?

Developing an assessment probe is different from creating appropriate questions for summative quizzes, tests, or state and national exams. The probes in this book were developed using the process described in *Mathematics Curriculum Topic Study: Bridging the Gap Between Standards and Practice* (Keeley & Rose, 2006). The process is summarized as follows:

- Identify the topic you plan to teach, and use national standards to examine concepts and specific ideas related to the topic. The national standards used to develop the probes for this book were NCTM's (2000) *Principles and Standards for School Mathematics* and the American Association for the Advancement of Science (AAAS)'s *Benchmarks for Science Literacy* (AAAS, 1993).

- Select the specific concepts or ideas you plan to address, and identify the relevant research findings. The source for research findings included NCTM's

Figure 1.6 Are They Equal? Probe

Use mental math to decide if the number sentence pairs are equal or not equal. Explain your thinking.

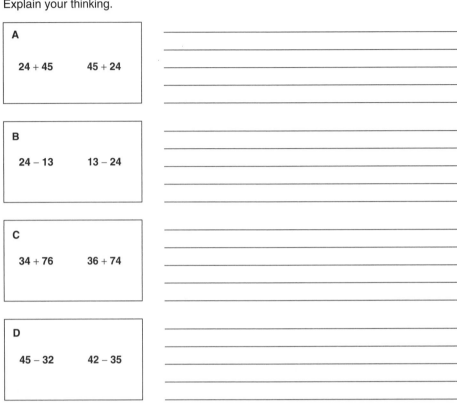

Research Companion to Principles and Standards for School Mathematics (2003), Chapter 15 of AAAS's *Benchmarks for Science Literacy*, and additional supplemental articles related to a topic.

• Focus on a concept or a specific idea you plan to address with the probe, and identify the related research findings. Choose the type of probe format that lends itself to the situation (see more information on probe format following the Gumballs in a Jar example). Develop the stem (the prompt), key (correct response), and distracters (incorrect responses derived from research findings) that match the developmental level of your students.

• Share your assessment probe(s) with colleagues for constructive feedback, pilot with students, and modify as needed.

Figure 1.7, which is taken from *Mathematics Curriculum Topic Study: Bridging the Gap Between Standards and Practice* (Keeley & Rose, 2006), provides the list of concepts and specific ideas related to the probability of simple events.

Figure 1.7   Probability Example

Topic: Probability (Simple Events)

Concepts and Ideas	Research Findings
• Events can be described in terms of being more or less likely, impossible, or certain. (*BSL,* Grades 3–5, p. 228)	**Understandings of Probability** (*Research Companion,* pp. 216–223)
• Probability is the measure of the likelihood of an event and can be represented by a number from 0 to 1. (*PSSM,* Grades 3–5, p. 176)	• Lack of understanding of ratio leads to difficulties in understanding of chance. • Students tend to focus on absolute rather than relative size.
• Understand that 0 represents the probability of an impossible event and 1 represents the probability of a certain event. (*PSSM,* Grades 3–5, p. 181)	• Although young children do not have a complete understanding of ratio, they have some intuitions of chance and randomness.
• Probabilities are ratios and can be expressed as fractions, percentages, or odds. (*BSL,* Grades 6–8, p. 229)	• A continuum of probabilistic thinking includes subjective, transitional, informal, quantitative, and numerical levels.
• Methods such as organized lists, tree diagrams, and area models are helpful in finding the number of possible outcomes. (*PSSM,* Grades 6–8, pp. 254–255)	• Third grade (approximately) is an appropriate place to begin systematic instruction. • "Equiprobability" is the notion that all outcomes are equally likely, disregarding relative and absolute size.
• The theoretical probability of a simple event can be found using the ratio of the number of favorable outcome/total possible outcomes. (*BSL,* Grades 6–8, p. 229)	• The outcome approach is defined as the misconception of predicting the outcome of an experiment rather than what is likely to occur. Typical responses to questions are "anything can happen."
• The probability of an outcome can be tested with simple experiments and simulations. (*PSSM,* Grades 6–8, pp. 254–255) • The relative frequency (experimental probability) can be computed using data generated from an experiment or simulation. (*PSSM,* Grades 6–8, pp. 254–255)	• Intuitive reasoning may lead to incorrect responses. Categories include representativeness and availability.
The experimental and theoretical probability of an event should be compared with discrepancies between predictions and outcomes from a large and representative sample taken seriously. (*PSSM,* Grades 6–8, pp. 254–255)	• Wording of task may influence reasoning. • NAEP results show fourth and eighth graders have difficulty with tasks involving probability as a ratio of "m chances out of n" but not with "1 chance out of n." • Increased understanding of sample space stems from multiple opportunities to determine and discuss possible outcomes and predict and test using simple experiments.
	Uncertainty (*BSL,* Chapter 15, p. 353)
	• Upper elementary students can give correct examples for certain, possible, and impossible events, but have difficulties calculating the probability of independent and dependent events.
	• Upper elementary students create "part to part" rather than "part to whole" relationships.

SOURCE: Keeley and Rose (2006).

The shaded information was used as the focus in the development of the probe, Gumballs in a Jar (see Figure 1.8). The probe is used to reveal *common errors* regarding probability, such as focusing on absolute size, or a lack of *conceptual* understanding of probability as a prediction of what is likely to happen. There is the same chance you will pick a black gumball out of each jar. Jar A has a probability of 3/5, and Jar B has a probability of 6/10 = 3/5. There are a (variety of trends in correct thinking related to this probe, some of which are doubling, ratios, and percents. Some students might correctly choose C but use incorrect reasoning such as "you can't know for sure since anything can happen," an explanation that indicates a lack of conceptual understanding of probability. Other students may demonstrate partial understanding with responses such as "each jar has more black than white."

Some students reason there are fewer white gumballs in Jar A compared to Jar B and therefore a better chance of picking a black gumball from Jar A. Others observe that Jar B has more black gumballs compared to Jar A and

Figure 1.8   Gumballs in a Jar Probe

Two jars hold black and white gumballs.

Jar A: 3 black and 2 white

Jar B: 6 black and 4 white

Jar A   **Jar B**

Which statement best describes the chance of getting a *black* gumball?

A. There is a better chance of getting a black gumball from Jar A

B. There is a better chance of getting a black gumball from Jar B

C. The chance of getting a black gumball is the same for both Jar A and Jar B

Explain your reason(s) for the statement you selected.

therefore reason that there is a better chance of picking a black gumball. In both cases, students are focusing on absolute size instead of relative size in comparing the likelihood of events. Students sometimes choose Distracter A due to an error in counting or calculation.

Additional probes can be written using the same list of concepts and specific ideas related to the probability of simple events. For example, by focusing on the statement from the research: National Assessment of Educational Progress results show fourth and eighth graders have difficulty with tasks involving probability as a ratio of "m chances out of n" but not with "1 chance out of n," a probe using an example of each can diagnose if students are demonstrating this difficulty.

WHAT IS THE STRUCTURE OF A MATHEMATICS ASSESSMENT PROBE?

The probes are designed to include two tiers, one for elicitation of common understandings and misunderstandings and the other for the elaboration of individual student thinking. Each of the tiers is described in more detail below.

Tier 1: Elicitation

Since the elicitation tier is designed to uncover common understandings and misunderstandings, a structured format using stems, correct answers, and distracters is used to narrow ideas found in the related research. The formats typically fall into one of four categories.

Selected Response

- One stem, one correct answer, and several distracters.

Figure 1.9   Selected Response

Which Is Bigger II

Use mental math and estimation to determine which problem results in the greatest answer.

A. $100 + (-34.2)$

B. $100 - (24.6)$

C. 100×0.52

D. $100 \div 0.24$

Multiple Selections Response

- Two or more sets of problems each with one stem, one correct answer, and one or more distracters.

Figure 1.10   Multiple Selections

Which Is Bigger?

Use mental math to answer each of the following:

a) 34×21 b) $34 \div 21$	a) 34×21 b) $34 \div 21$
Circle One:	**Circle One:**
a is bigger b is bigger	a is bigger b is bigger
a and b are equal	a and b are equal

a) 34×21 b) $34 \div 21$	a) $.21 \times .34$ b) $.21 \div .34$
Circle One:	**Circle One:**
a is bigger b is bigger	a is bigger b is bigger
a and b are equal	a and b are equal

Opposing Views/Answers

- Two or more statements are provided and students are asked to choose the statement they agree with.

Figure 1.11   Opposing Views

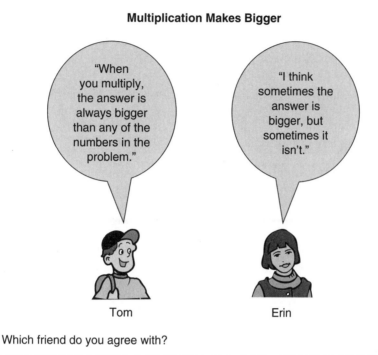

Multiplication Makes Bigger

"When you multiply, the answer is always bigger than any of the numbers in the problem."

Tom

"I think sometimes the answer is bigger, but sometimes it isn't."

Erin

Which friend do you agree with?

This format is adapted from *Concept Cartoons in Education,* created by Brenda Keogh and Stuart Naylor for probing student ideas in science (Naylor & Keogh, 2000).

Examples and Nonexamples List

- Several examples and non-examples are given and students are asked to check only the examples based on a given statement.

Figure 1.12   Examples

Using mental math, indicate which problems result in a positive answer.

A. -(-53 + 92)   B. -34 - 27

C. 93 - (-56)   D. (-24)(35)

E. $\dfrac{-5 - 10}{-(-2)}$ F. (-34)(-54)

G. -34 + -56   H. $\dfrac{-5}{-2}$

Tier 2: Elaboration

The second tier of each of the probes is designed for individual elaboration of the reasoning used to respond to the question asked in the first tier. Mathematics teachers gain a wealth of information by delving into the thinking behind students' answers, not just when answers are wrong but also when they are correct (Burns, 2005). Although the Tier 1 answers and distracters are designed around common understandings and misunderstandings, the elaboration tier allows educators to look more deeply at student thinking. Often a student chooses a specific response, correct or incorrect, for an atypical reason. Also, there are many different ways to approach a problem correctly; therefore, the elaboration tier allows educators to look for trends in thinking and in methods used.

WHAT ADDITIONAL INFORMATION IS PROVIDED WITH EACH MATHEMATICS ASSESSMENT PROBE?

In *Designing Professional Development for Teachers of Science and Mathematics*, Loucks-Horsley, Love, Stiles, Mundry, and Hewson (2003) describe action research as an effective professional development strategy. To use the probes in this manner, it is important to consider the complete implementation process. We refer to an action research QUEST as working through the full cycle of:

Figure 1.13   QUEST Cycle

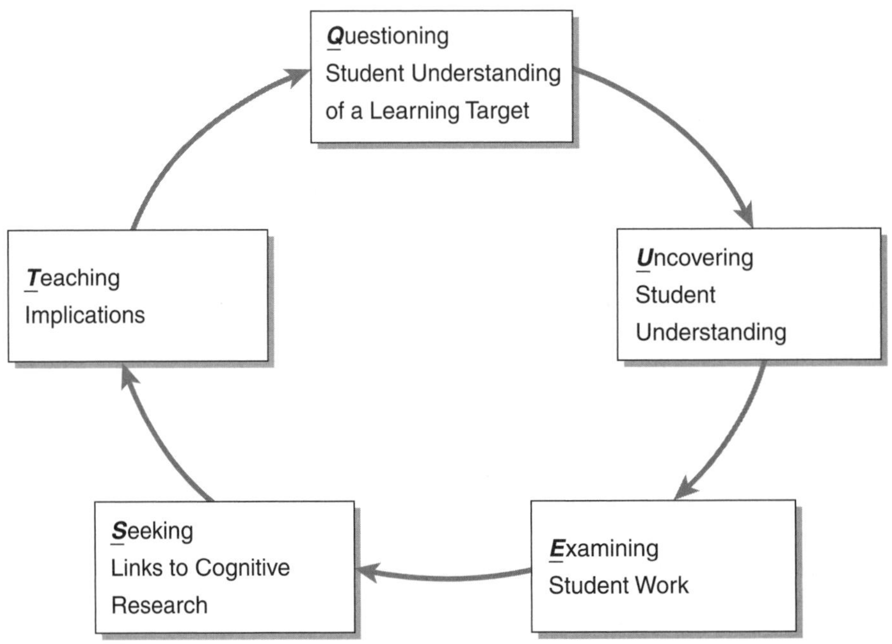

- *Questioning student understanding of a particular concept*

- *Uncovering understanding and misunderstandings using a probe*

- *Examining student work*

- *Seeking links to cognitive research to drive next steps in instruction*

- *Teaching implications based on findings and determining impact on learning by asking an additional question.*

The Teachers' Notes, included with each probe, have been designed around the action research QUEST cycle, and each set of notes includes relevant information for each component of the cycle (see Figure 1.13). These components are described in detail.

Questioning student understanding of a particular concept. This component helps to focus a teacher on what a particular probe elicits and to provide information on grade-appropriate knowledge. Figure 1.14 shows an example Question from the Mathematics Assessment Probe, Gumballs in a Jar.

Figure 1.14   Questioning Student Understanding

In thinking about probability, do students have a solid understanding of part-whole relationships?

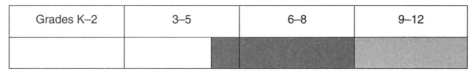

Grades K–2	3–5	6–8	9–12

Grade Level for "Gumballs in Jar" Probe

Grade span bars are provided to indicate the developmentally appropriate level of mathematics as aligned to the NCTM standards and cognitive research. The dark gray band represents the grade levels where the mathematics required of the probe is aligned to the standards, and the lighter gray band shows where field-testing has indicated students still have difficulties.

Uncovering understanding by giving the Mathematics Assessment Probe to students. Figure 1.15 shows an example Uncovering Understanding from the Mathematics Assessment Probe, Gumballs in a Jar.

Figure 1.15   Uncovering Understandings

Gumballs in a Jar Content Standard: Data Analysis and Probability
Variations: Gumballs in a Jar II
(one jar for Grades 3 through 5) and Gumballs in a Jar III
(nondoubling variation for Grades 7 through 12)

Examining student work. This section includes information about the stem, answer(s), and distracters as related to the research on cognitive learning. Example student responses are given for a selected number of elicited understandings and misunderstandings. The categories, *conceptual/procedural* and *common errors/overgeneralizations* are used where appropriate and are written in bold italics. Figure 1.16 shows an example Examining Student Work from the Mathematics Assessment Probe, Gumballs in a Jar.

Figure 1.16 Examining Student Work

The distracters may reveal *common errors* regarding probability, such as focusing on absolute size, or a lack of *conceptual* understanding of probability as a prediction of what is likely to happen.

- *The correct answer is C.* There is the same chance you will pick a black gumball out of each jar. Jar A has a probability of 3/5 and Jar B has a probability of 6/10 = 3/5. There are a variety of trends in correct thinking related to this probe, some of which are doubling, ratios, and percents. Some students might correctly choose C with incorrect reasoning such as, "You can't know for sure since anything can happen," which indicates lack of *conceptual* understanding of probability. Other students may demonstrate partial understanding with responses such as "Each jar has more black than white."
- *Distracter A:* Some students reason that there are fewer white gumballs in Jar A compared to Jar B and therefore a better chance of picking a black gumball from Jar A. These students focus on absolute size instead of relative size in comparing the likelihood of events. Students sometimes choose Distracter A due to an error in counting or calculation.
- *Distracter B:* Students observe Jar B as having more black gumballs compared to Jar A and conclude that there is a better chance of picking a black gumball. These students focus on absolute size instead of relative size in comparing the likelihood of events.

Note: Typical student responses that are examples of these results are provided at the end of each actual probe. The Gumballs in a Jar probe is on page 122.

Seeking links to cognitive research. This section provides additional information about research that teachers can use for further study of the topic. Figure 1.17 shows an example from the Mathematics Assessment Probe, Gumballs in a Jar.

Figure 1.17 Seeking Links to Cognitive Research

[Jones, Langrall, Thorton, and Mogill] theorized that children exhibit four levels of thinking about probability situations: subjective, transitional, informal quantitative, and numerical. (NCTM, 2003, p. 217)

[The Outcome Approach]: Students might not possess a process model for chance experiments because they do not envision the results of a single trial of an experiment as just one of many possible outcomes that will vary across a sample space if the experiment is repeated. (NCTM, 2003, p. 218)

Teaching implications. Being aware of student difficulties and the sources of those difficulties is important, but designing instruction is most important to help diminish those difficulties. Although some ideas are included, the authors strongly encourage educators to use the Curriculum Topic Study (CTS) process to search for additional teaching implications. Each set of Teachers' Notes includes the related CTS Guide for further study, additional references, and a "teacher sound bite" from a field-tester of the probe. Figure 1.18 shows an example from the Mathematics Assessment Probe, Gumballs in a Jar.

Figure 1.18   Teaching Implications

To support a deeper understanding for students in middle school in regard to probability, the following are ideas and questions to consider in conjunction with the research.

Focus Through Instruction

- Students should learn about probability as a measurement of the likelihood of events
- Students should explore probability through experiments that have only a few outcomes
- Computer simulations provide a quick method of collecting large samples in providing experimental data that is close to the theoretical probability
- To correct misconceptions, it is helpful for students to make predictions and then compare the predictions with actual outcomes
- Students should encounter the idea that although they can't determine an individual outcome, they can predict the frequency of various outcomes
- A solid understanding of ratio and proportion is critical for understanding relative frequency
- In Grades 3 through 5, students should use common fractions to represent the probability of a certain event

Questions to Consider . . . When Working With
Students As They Grapple With the Idea of Probability

- Do the students focus on relative size when calculating probabilities?
- Do students view probability as a prediction of what is likely to happen?
- Over time, are students able to make predictions based on what is likely to happen?

Additional References for Research and Teaching Implications:

NCTM (1993b), *Research Ideas for the Classroom, High School Mathematics*, pp. 177–194.

NCTM (1993c), *Research Ideas for the Classroom, Middle Grades Mathematics*, pp. 6, 83–87.

NCTM (2000), *Principles and Standards for School Mathematics*, pp. 181, 254.

NCTM (2003), *Research Companion to Principles and Standards for School Mathematics*, p. 217.

Stavy & Tirosh (2000), *How Students (Mis-) Understand Science and Mathematics*, pp. 1–2, 23–24.

Curriculum Topic Study

Related CTS Guide:
Probability

Following the Teachers' Notes and sample student responses, adaptations and/or variations to the Mathematics Assessment Probe are provided for some of the probes. *Variations* to the probe provide a different structure (selected response, multiple selections, opposing views, or examples/nonexamples) for the question within the same grade span. An *Adaptation* to the probe is similar in content to the original, but the level of mathematics changes for use at a different grade span.

In addition to the Teachers' Notes, a Note Template is included in Resource A. The Note Template provides a structured approach to working through a probe QUEST. The components of the template are described in Figure 1.19.

WHAT MATHEMATICS ASSESSMENT PROBES ARE INCLUDED IN THE BOOK?

Many of the samples included in this book fall into the Number and Operations content strand because the cognitive research is abundant within this area. The book also includes multiple examples for the following additional content standards: Algebra, Data Analysis, Probability, Geometry, and Measurement. Figure 1.20 provides an "at a glance" look of the grade span and content of the probes included in Chapters 3 through 5.

Grade span bars are provided to indicate the developmentally appropriate level of mathematics as aligned to NCTM standards as well as the cognitive research.

An important note to high school teachers: Many of the mathematics expectations in the Grades 6–8 span of the NCTM standards are being introduced to some students for the first time in high school mathematics courses. For example, the Are They Linear? probe assesses whether students are able to identify linear relationships when represented in different symbolic forms. This content is typical of a first-year high school mathematics course. In addition, research shows high school students, college students, and even many adults have misunderstandings similar to those of middle school students. The gray band represents probes that align to topics taught at an earlier level but are appropriate for high school use.

Figure 1.19   Note Template

*Q*uestioning for student understanding

*U*ncovering understandings

Adaptations made to the probe:

*E*xamining student work

*S*eeking links to cognitive research

    Source:

    Findings:

    Source:

    Findings:

    Source:

    Findings:

*T*eaching implications

    Source:

    Findings:

    Source:

    Findings:

    Source:

    Findings:

Summary of instructional implications/plan of action:

Results of instruction:

Figure 1.20   Mathematics Assessment Probes

Key

▓▓▓	Target for Instruction Based on National Standards and Cognitive Research
░░░	Prerequisite Concept/Field Testing Indicates Student Difficulty

Question	Probe	Grade Span Bars			
		K–2	3–5	6–8	9–12
Chapter 3: Number and Operations					
What do students understand about magnitude versus quantity?	Is One Group More?	▓ Target			
What do students understand about our number system and place value?	Building Numbers	▓ Target	░ Prereq		
What do students understand about the commutative and associative properties as they relate to the numbers used in addition and subtraction equations?	Are They Equal?	▓ Target	▓ Target		
What do students understand about part-whole relationships in identifying fractional parts?	Fractional Parts		▓ Target	░ Prereq	
Do students consider place value when comparing the size of decimals?	Comparing Decimals		▓ Target	░ Prereq	
What do students understand about part-whole relationships when comparing fractions?	Comparing Fractions		▓ Target	░ Prereq	
When simplifying expressions, do students follow the rules for the order of operations?	Order of Operations			▓ Target	░ Prereq
Do students understand the effect of multiplication and division on different numbers?	Which Is Bigger?			▓ Target	░ Prereq
Do students have an understanding of the meaning and effect of operations with negative numbers?	Are You Positive?			▓ Target	░ Prereq
Are students able to accurately estimate a percent of a number?	What Percent Is That?			▓ Target	░ Prereq
Chapter 4: Algebra, Data Analysis, and Probability					
What does the equals sign mean?	It's All About Balance	▓ Target	░ Prereq		
Do students understand that the equals sign symbolizes equivalence?	Seesaw	▓ Target	░ Prereq		
Do students accurately use symbolic representation to make sense of the relationship being described?	Students Versus Teachers			▓ Target	░ Prereq
In thinking about rate of change graphically, do students understand how scale affects the presentation of a graph?	Rate of Change (Slope)			▓ Target	░ Prereq
Are students able to identify linear relationships when represented symbolically?	Are They Linear?			▓ Target	░ Prereq
Do students interpret graphs as literal pictures?	Distance From Home			▓ Target	░ Prereq
In thinking about probability, do students have a solid understanding of part-whole relationships?	Gumballs in a Jar		▓ Target	░ Prereq	
Are students able to apply the concepts of compound probability?	The Spinners				▓ Target
Chapter 5: Geometry and Measurement					
What do students understand about the attributes of a triangle?	What Does a Triangle Look Like?	▓ Target	░ Prereq		
What do students understand about properties of a rectangle and their relationship to a square?	What Does a Rectangle Look Like?	▓ Target	▓ Target		
What do students understand and not understand about linear measurement?	How Long Is the Pencil?	░ Prereq	▓ Target		
Do students perceive the length of an angle's rays as having an effect on the angle's measure?	Comparing Angles			▓ Target	░ Prereq
Do students accurately compare the volume and surface area of a box before and after dividing it into four boxes?	Box Cutting/ Comparing Volume and Surface Area			▓ Target	
Are students familiar with the attributes of parallelograms?	Parallelograms			▓ Target	░ Prereq
Do students understand how to find the volume of a box, given the side lengths or given the area of a face and the length of the other side?	Volume of a Box			▓ Target	░ Prereq

2

Instructional Implications

An important first step for making classroom assessment work is to understand the difference between assessment and evaluation. Some people use the terms assessment and evaluation interchangeably, but they have different meanings. When we assess, we are gathering information about student learning that informs our teaching and helps students learn more. We may teach differently, based on what we find as we assess. When we evaluate, we decide whether or not students have learned what they needed to learn and how well they have learned it. (Davies, 2000, p. 1)

Mathematics Assessment Probes represent one approach to diagnostic assessment. They can be used for formative assessment purposes if the information about students' understandings and misunderstandings is used to focus instruction. Purposes for using the Mathematics Assessment Probes included in this chapter are:

- differentiating instruction
- assessing point of entry
- analyzing trends in thinking
- giving student interviews
- promoting student-to-student dialogue
- allowing for individual think time
- improving students' process skills
- assessing effectiveness of instructional activities
- moving beyond the individual classroom

Each of the contexts is briefly described, and in some cases, images from practice are used to highlight strategies within the contexts. The images from practice provide a window into the classroom of a teacher who uses the Mathematics Assessment Probes in the classroom.

DIFFERENTIATING INSTRUCTION

Diagnostic assessments provide information to assist teacher planning and guide differentiated instruction. (McTighe & O'Connor, 2005, p. 11)

Differentiation is an organized yet flexible way of proactively adjusting teaching and learning to meet students where they are and to help all students meet maximum growth as learners (Tomlinson, 1999). Differentiation looks dissimilar across classrooms as educators incorporate different strategies, including varying the size of the numbers within a problem set, reducing the number of assigned problems, or allowing the use of tools. The important consideration in differentiating instruction is to allow all students access to an "excellent and equitable mathematics program that provides solid support for their learning and is responsive to their prior knowledge, intellectual strengths, and personal interests" (NCTM, 2000, p. 13).

The following Image From Practice highlights how a teacher used the information from a probe to plan instruction so that all students could learn the same concept even if some required various methods of intervention along the way.

Image From Practice: Are They Equal?

After giving my third grade students "Are They Equal?" (see Chapter 3), I was able to quickly assess the levels of understanding demonstrated. A few students understood that the commutative property holds for addition but not subtraction and were able to communicate this understanding in relationship to the properties of addition and subtraction. About half of the class could choose *equal* versus *not equal* correctly but could not go beyond solving the problem to communicate their reasoning. Many students also incorrectly thought both the addition and the subtraction sets were equal. One particular student's thinking really captured my attention. I could see she had done the computation correctly, yet she made conclusions about equality that were puzzling. She summarized that equality was decided by the digit in the one's place, which indicated whether the answer was odd or even. Her justification was that "even numbers are equal and odd numbers are not equal."

Next Steps:

One instructional target of the unit is to have students consider the relationship of the numbers used in problems prior to just applying a procedure. I needed to consider students' prior knowledge in order to develop deeper understanding for each student in the class.

For the students who already had this understanding, I pushed them to think about how the commutative property is helpful when adding multiple number sets and with larger numbers.

I discovered that of the students who answered correctly after computing, some of them could apply the concept but thought they should complete the calculation. For those who were unable to think about the property without calculating, I paid particular attention to providing multiple examples, leading to a discussion on the patterns presented.

The students who still considered 24 − 13 equal to 13 − 24 provided a different challenge. While providing opportunities for multiple examples, we went back to modeling the process on the 100's chart and number line. Having the opportunity to hear from other students was an important component in pushing this group's understanding.

My goal for the student who overgeneralized from working with even and odd numbers was to work with her to build an understanding of the concept of equality by bringing out the balance and using linking cubes which represented the sum of two numbers. In addition, I gave her more opportunities to work with the idea of odd and even numbers and to make connections to identify when it is helpful mathematically to use that information about numbers (i.e., division).

ASSESSING POINT OF ENTRY

While teachers may fully grasp the importance of working with students' prior conceptions, they need to know the typical conceptions of students with respect to the topic about to be taught. (National Research Council [NRC], 2005, p. 20)

Assessing prior knowledge is a key first step in using assessment to inform teaching. Often, assumptions are made about what students do or do not know. Assumptions about lack of readiness may be based on teachers' experiences with student lack of understanding in previous years. Assumptions that students are ready are often based on the fact that the students have studied the materials before (Stepans, Schmidt, Welsh, Reins, & Saigo, 2005).

Because of these assumptions, the mathematics concepts of an instructional unit are sometimes beyond students' readiness. Just as prevalent is wasting valuable classroom time by incorporating activities below the instructional level of the students. The Mathematics Assessment Probes can be given prior to a specific unit of investigation to gauge the starting point and allow teachers to make decisions based on evidence rather than assumption.

ANALYZING TRENDS IN STUDENT THINKING

Compiling an inventory for a set of papers can provide a sense of the class's progress and thus inform decisions about how to differentiate instruction. (Burns, 2005, p. 29)

In her recent article, "Looking at How Students Reason," Marilyn Burns describes a process for taking a classroom inventory:

After asking a class of 27 fifth graders to circle the larger fraction—$^2/_3$ or ¾—and explain their reasoning, I reviewed their papers and listed the strategies they used. Their strategies included drawing pictures (either circles or rectangles); changing to fractions with common denominators ($^8/_{12}$ and $^9/_{12}$); seeing which fraction was closer to 1 ($^2/_3$ is $^1/_3$ away, but $^3/_4$ is only $^1/_4$ away); and relating the fractions to money ($^2/_3$ of $1.00 is about 66 cents, whereas $^3/_4$ of $1.00 is 75 cents). Four of the students were unable to compare the two fractions correctly. I now had direction for future lessons that would provide interventions for the struggling students and give all the students opportunities to learn different strategies from one another. (p. 29)

Developing this "sense of the class" allows for instructional decision making. The probes can be used for this purpose by categorizing student responses and asking the following questions:

What are the primary methods students used for solving this problem?

How often do the primary methods result in the correct response?

Which of the methods is generalizable?

What student methods are considered outliers?

Which of the primary methods are more efficient?

Based on the sense of the class, what instructional strategies are effective for this particular learning target?

The last question is an important one because "students' preconceptions must be addressed explicitly in order for them to change their existing understanding and beliefs. If students' initial ideas are ignored, the understanding that they develop can be very different from what the teacher intends" (Stepans et al., 2005, p. 35).

GIVING STUDENT INTERVIEWS

Interviewing provides the opportunity to talk with students—that is, to hear their explanations and to pose follow-up questions that probe the rationale behind their beliefs. (Stepans et al., 2005, p. 36)

Giving student interviews is an important and useful strategy for several purposes.

The main purpose for interviewing a student is to probe that student's mathematical thinking. By interviewing a variety of students in a class, [teachers] can get a better sense of the range of thinking in that class. Interviewing takes time, but the potential payoff is great for helping make sense of students' responses to questions. (Bright & Joyner, 2004, p. 184)

The following Image From Practice highlights how a teacher used a probe (What Does a Triangle Look Like?) as a tool to "interview" students.

Image From Practice: Triangles

I used the Triangles probe for one of my math centers. I cut out each of the shapes provided on the probe and added a few additional shapes of my own. I made four sets of the cards and gave one set to each student (I have four students working at each center). I asked each student to look at the cards and make a pile of triangles and a pile of shapes that are NOT triangles. Working with a small group provided me the opportunity to watch each student as he/she made a decision about where to place a card. Based on some of the choices made, I then asked the students questions about the placement of the shapes. I was able to cycle all students through the center within the 2 days planned for this particular set of center activities.

PROMOTING STUDENT-TO-STUDENT DIALOGUE

A focus on student thinking requires classroom norms that encourage the expression of ideas (tentative and certain, partially and fully informed, as well as risk taking). It requires that mistakes be viewed not as revelations of inadequacy, but as helpful contributions in the search for understanding. (NRC, 2005, p. 20)

The Mathematics Assessment Probes can be used as conversation starters for class discussions. These conversation starters can promote both conflict and collaboration as students work to validate answers and refine their thinking based on their peers' justifications.

The following Image From Practice highlights how a teacher used a probe, Gumballs in a Jar, to address a misunderstanding typical of students at a prior grade span.

Image From Practice: Gumballs in a Jar

Before moving into a unit on compound probability, Mr. Peters was interested in how his freshman Integrated Math students approached problems involving simple probability. He gave his students a handout with the Gumballs in a Jar probe on both the front and back of the paper. After giving students time to complete the elicitation tier, he asked students to put the letter of their response on a sticky note, and he collected these as students worked on the elaboration tier of the probe. Mr. Peters quickly created a bar graph with the sticky notes as a visual display of the individual responses. After students finished with the elaboration of their thought process, he led a class discussion, with students justifying their choice by describing their reasoning.

(Continued)

(Continued)

> Without giving the correct answer away, Mr. Peters closed the activity by asking students to turn over the handout to the "fresh" Gumballs in a Jar task and to answer the question based on the preceding discussion. In comparing the before and after responses, he was pleased to note a change from an incorrect response to a correct response in all but one of the students. In addition to the change to the correct response, he also noted an increase in sophistication of the explanations, with the majority of the students using ratios or percents to justify their reasoning. Mr. Peters felt the group as a whole was ready to proceed to the compound probability unit.
>
> This process allows students to practice metacognition, thinking about one's own thinking. When asked to redo the problem based on the discussion that followed individual process time, students are forced to think about their original ideas and how they may or may not have changed.

ALLOWING FOR INDIVIDUAL THINK TIME

A problem with traditional questioning is that the teacher gets to hear only one student's thinking. (Leahy, Lyon, Thompson, & Wiliam, 2005, p. 22)

Eliciting student ideas using a Mathematics Assessment Probe allows for individual students to express their *initial* thinking—the first phase of eliciting student thinking—without the interference of other students' thought processes. Although student conversation about the learning target addressed in the probe is important, the conversation does not necessarily need to occur by having students discuss the probe. Often, the student conversation takes place during activities specifically chosen to meet the needs of the students, based on evidence of understanding uncovered by the probe.

The following excerpt from the article, "Classroom Assessment: Minute by Minute, Day by Day," provides additional ideas for allowing for individual think time. The strategies described below can be incorporated while using a Mathematics Assessment Probe.

> Teachers can also use questions to check on student understanding before continuing the lesson. We call this a "hinge point" in the lesson because the lesson can go in different directions, depending on student responses. By explicitly integrating these hinge points into instruction, teachers can make their teaching more responsive to their students' needs in real time.
>
> However, no matter how good the hinge-point question, the traditional model of classroom questioning presents two additional problems. The first is lack of engagement. If the classroom rule dictates that students raise their hands to answer questions, then students can disengage from the classroom by keeping their hands down.

The second problem with traditional questioning is that the teacher gets to hear only one student's thinking. To gauge the understanding of the whole class, the teacher needs to get responses from all the students in real time. One way to do this is to have all students write their answers on individual dry-erase boards, which they hold up at the teacher's request. The teacher can then scan responses for novel solutions as well as misconceptions.

Another approach is to give each student a set of four cards labeled A, B, C, and D, and ask the question in multiple-choice format. If the question is well designed, the teacher can quickly judge the different levels of understanding in the class. If all students answer correctly, the teacher can move on. If no one answers correctly, the teacher might choose to re-teach the concept. If some students answer correctly and some answer incorrectly, the teacher can use that knowledge to engineer a whole-class discussion on the concept or match up the students for peer teaching. Hinge-point questions provide a window into students' thinking and, at the same time, give the teacher some ideas about how to take the students' learning forward. (Leahy et al., 2005, p. 22)

IMPROVING STUDENTS' PROCESS SKILLS

Examining and discussing both exemplary and problematic pieces of mathematics writing can be beneficial at all levels. (NCTM, 2000, p. 62)

Although the primary purpose of a Mathematics Assessment Probe is to elicit understandings, partial understandings, and misunderstandings, a secondary benefit is the improvement of students' written communication skills. After instruction and discussion of the underlying mathematics, individual student responses to a probe can be critiqued for clarity, correct information, and coherency.

The following Image From Practice highlights how a teacher used a probe (Are They Equal?), to improve students' methods of justification.

Image From Practice: Are They Equal?

Prior to our work with adding and subtracting two-digit numbers, I gave my second grade class the Are They Equal? probe to diagnose student prior knowledge of composing and decomposing numbers to check for equality. Our curriculum material, which is constructivist in nature, allows multiple opportunities for students to develop their own algorithms and methods for computing. Students progress from using manipulatives, 200 charts, and open number lines to a paper-pencil procedure. At the end of the unit, I gave my students an Are They Equal? probe and asked them once again to answer the questions (I am always amazed at the number of students who don't recall working on the problem previously).

(Continued)

(Continued)

> We have a class discussion of what constitutes a "good" explanation, using the communication criteria of our problem-solving rubric, and students have a chance to add to their work based on our discussion. After reviewing student work, I choose several responses to write on chart paper for a final critique of the responses. I find this process beneficial for students to understand the importance of using properties of numbers as well as examples in justifying their thinking (for example: 23 + 45 is equal to 25 + 43 because 20 + 40 + 3 + 5 is equal to 20 + 40 + 5 + 3. The order you add the tens and the ones doesn't matter).

ASSESSING EFFECTIVENESS OF INSTRUCTIONAL ACTIVITIES

In planning individual lessons, teachers should strive to organize the mathematics so that fundamental ideas form an integrated whole. (NCTM, 2000, p. 15)

Using probes in a pre- and post-assessment format allows for evaluation of curriculum and instruction. When implementing a new or revised set of activities, evaluating the impact of those activities on student learning is an important component of analyzing the effectiveness of the activities and making further revisions. In using Mathematics Assessment Probes for this purpose, it is important to consider the conceptual understanding or mathematical "big ideas" that are addressed within the activities.

The following Image From Practice highlights how a teacher used a probe, Student Versus Teachers, after implementing an instructional unit to assess an increase in students' understanding of using variables to represent relationships.

Image From Practice: Students Versus Teachers

After learning about probes from our involvement with a State Math and Science Partnership project, I decided to try using a probe with my seventh grade heterogeneous mathematics group as a pre- and postassessment for a module of instruction in our newly adopted program. Prior to our unit on writing and evaluating variable expressions, I gave the class the Students Versus Teachers probe and collected their work. I reviewed the work to assess the point of entry and found the majority of the students were able to correctly answer the addition problem, but very few understood the relationship involving multiplication. Using Post-its, I marked my textbook indicating areas where I could speed up and where I would like to spend more time. I also highlighted key questions within the student questions that would require students to think about the relationship of the variables and test the relationship of the equation using sample numbers.

Two and a half weeks later, after moving through the related activities, I handed back the papers and asked the students to review their previous answers and explanations. After the students reworked their solutions and explanations, I collected the papers to look for correct answers, key terminology, and strategies for checking for reasonableness. I was pleased to see the difference in the thinking of my students! Since we use a spiral program, we will revisit this idea at a deeper level in another 5 weeks, so I made a note in my planner of the students who still were demonstrating difficulty and plan to revisit the ideas with them prior to reaching the next level. Using the probe allowed me to focus on the big idea of the unit and not get caught up in supplementing individual activities.

MOVING BEYOND THE INDIVIDUAL CLASSROOM

The engine of improvement, growth and renewal in a professional learning community is collective inquiry. The people in such a school are relentless in questioning the status quo, seeking new methods, testing those methods, and then reflecting on the results. (Dufour, 2001)

Another important opportunity provided by using the probes is examining student work with other educators.

The most important aspect of this strategy is that teachers have access to and then develop for themselves the ability to understand the content students are struggling with and ways that they, the teachers, can help. Pedagogical content knowledge—that special province of excellent teachers—is absolutely necessary for teachers to maximize their learning as they examine and discuss what students demonstrate they know and do not know. (Loucks-Horsley et al. 2003, p. 183)

By providing a link to Curriculum Topic Study (Keeley & Rose, 2006) as well as to resources with additional research and instructional implications specific to the ideas of the probe, Mathematics Assessment Probes provide a means for a collaborative approach to examining student thinking and planning for improving instruction.

The following Image From Practice highlights how a teacher used a probe (Which Is Bigger?), to address a typical student overgeneralization with other mathematics teachers at her school.

Image From Practice: Which Is Bigger?

I introduced the probes to my teaching colleagues (sixth through eighth grade), and we agreed to give the Which Is Bigger? probe to see if our students held the common misconception, "multiplication makes bigger." We were definitely surprised at the number of students who so quickly answered exactly what the research was indicating! This revelation prompted us to review our curriculum units across the grade levels to see how the idea builds within our district program.

Our program had many of the hands-on activities suggested in the standards such as using grid paper and using measurement as a context, so why were students holding onto to this belief? As a group, we developed questions and reflection prompts to accompany each of the related units. We also agreed to require more mental math and estimation prior to finding the exact answer. Our conversations revealed that the issue wasn't stemming from our written curriculum but rather from our instruction. Tackling this through examining student work created an environment that felt safe and resulted in a "no finger-pointing" conversation.

Imagine our surprise when a few months later we were examining our state test (from last year's eighth-grade students) and we came across a problem eliciting the same idea. We weren't surprised that our former students and students statewide did poorly on the problem. We now plan to take the problem, add "explain your choice," and give the item as a follow-up probe to our sixth through eighth-grade students at the end of the year in order to assess progress.

SUMMARY

In *How Students Learn: Mathematics in the Classroom*, the National Research Council (2005) describes a use of assessment as follows:

> Assessments are a central feature of both a learner-centered and a knowledge-centered classroom. They permit the teacher to grasp students' preconceptions, which is critical to working with and building on those notions. (p. 16)

The purposes this chapter described for using Mathematics Assessment Probes represent the multiple ways the probes can support educators in "engaging students' preconceptions and building on existing knowledge" and developing an "assessment–centered classroom environment" (NRC, 2005).

Number and Operations Assessment Probes

Key

■ (dark)	Target for Instruction Based on National Standards and Cognitive Research
░ (light)	Prerequisite Concept/Field Testing Indicates Student Difficulty

Question	Probe	Grade Span Bars			
		K–2	3–5	6–8	9–12
Chapter 3: Number and Operations					
What do students understand about magnitude versus quantity?	Is One Group More?	■			
What do students understand about our number system and place value?	Building Numbers	■	░		
What do students understand about the commutative and associative properties as they relate to the numbers used in addition and subtraction equations?	Are They Equal?	■	■	░	
What do students understand about part-whole relationships in identifying fractional parts?	Fractional Parts		■	░	
Do students consider place value when comparing the size of decimals?	Comparing Decimals		░	■	
What do students understand about part-whole relationships when comparing fractions?	Comparing Fractions		■	░	
When simplifying expressions, do students follow the rules for the order of operations?	Order of Operations			■	░
Do students understand the effect of multiplication and division on different numbers?	Which Is Bigger?			■	░
Do students have an understanding of the meaning and effect of operations with negative numbers?	Are You Positive?			■	░
Are students able to accurately estimate a percent of a number?	What Percent Is That?			■	░

Probe 1

IS ONE GROUP MORE?

Group A	Group B

Does one group have more smiley faces? How do you know?

_____

_____

_____

_____

_____

_____

_____

TEACHERS' NOTES: IS ONE GROUP MORE?

Grade Level for "Is One Group More?" Probe

Grades K–2	3–5	6–8	9–12
███████			

Questioning for Student Understanding

What do students understand about magnitude versus quantity?

Uncovering Understandings

Is One Group More? Content Standard: Number and Operations
Variation: Ducks in a Row

Examining Student Work

The distracters may reveal *common errors* and lack of conceptual knowledge regarding the idea of magnitude.

- *The correct answer is A.* Students who choose A are looking at the quantity of both groups and are not being distracted by the larger size of the objects. (See Students 3 and 4 in *Student Responses* section.)
- *Students who answer B.* Students who choose B are most likely paying more attention to the larger smiley faces, which look like "more" in regard to occupied space. (See Students 1 and 2 in *Student Responses* section.)

Seeking Links to Cognitive Research

Understanding number requires much more than verbal counting. It also includes the ability to determine the total number of objects and reasoning about that numerosity using number relationships. Numerosity and reasoning are influenced by the size of the numbers and the ability to think using groups. Since numbers are used in a variety of ways and with a variety of symbols, context and symbols are an added influence on children's understanding of number. (NCTM, 1993a, p. 44)

Piaget (1952/1965) studied children's dependence on length and density when they are asked to compare the number of objects in two rows containing the same number of objects. Young children (until about 5 or 6) only paid attention to the relative length of the two rows. Rows of the same length were said to have the same number of objects; otherwise, *the longer row* was said to be *more numerous* than the shorter row. Some older children based their judgments on the relative density of the two rows, stating that *the denser row was more numerous.* These two responses are in line with the intuitive rule "More A (length of row/density of row)— More B (number of objects)." (Stavy & Tirosh, 2000, pp. 13–14)

Magnitude involves activities such as describing the global magnitude of the objects, making direct or side-by-side comparison of objects, or making magnitude judgments with or without quantification. For example, Briana brings a newspaper and puts it on an art table. Amy says to her, "This isn't big enough to cover the table." Abdul and Michael build structures with Legos. Abdul says to Michael, "Look at mine. Mine is big!" Michael says, "Mine is bigger!" They place their Lego structures side by side and compare whose is taller. (Clements & Sarama, 2004, p. 94)

By the age of 4, most children can also compare two stacks of chips that differ in height in obvious, perceptually salient ways and tell which pile has more or less. Children who can do this can solve the same problem when the question is phrased "Which pile is bigger (or smaller)?" and can solve similar problems involving comparisons of length (when the chips are aligned along a table) and of weight (when the chips are placed on a balance scale), provided the differences between the sets are visually obvious. (NRC, 2005, p. 272)

Understanding number is a precursor to calculating effectively and flexibly with the base ten number system. The concept of number develops over several years, generally between ages 2 and 8. Besides being able to count accurately to find "how many," it is very important that children develop number sense, an ability to know how large a number is in comparison to other numbers. (Bay Area Mathematics Task Force, 1999, p. 7)

The concepts and skills related to number and operations are a major emphasis of mathematics instruction in pre-kindergarten through Grade 2. During the early years teachers must help students strengthen their sense of number, moving from the initial development of basic counting techniques to more sophisticated understanding of the size of numbers, number relationships, patterns, operations, and place value. (NCTM, 2000, p. 79)

*T*eaching Implications

In order to support a deeper understanding for students in elementary school in regard to quantity, specifically with understanding the difference between quantity and magnitude, the following are ideas and questions to consider in conjunction with the research.

Focus Through Instruction

- Pay careful attention to children's ability to count
- Help students shift representations when counting to numerals
- Give practice in instant recognition of small quantities (e.g., subitizing)
- Connect numbers with their use as real-world quantities
- Build up students' intuitive sense of "which has more"
- Lead students to compare the quantities represented, rather than the digits, when working with relative magnitude
- Make direct comparisons between quantities and size by asking students about the relationship
- Offer experiences that encourage students to reason about the numerosity of a collection
- Use explicit language during instruction to refer to the comparison of collections of objects in terms of quantity
- Emphasize moving students from initial forward-number word sequence (counting one, two, three . . .) to an understanding of the size of numbers
- Discuss number relationships when counting collections (e.g., cardinal and ordinal significance)
- Provide opportunities for students to have conversations about their conjectures about quantity
- Use specific language to describe objects that relate to size and quantity to help students develop their mathematical vocabulary when describing objects (e.g., my box of crayons is big in referring to the size of the box instead of the quantity of the crayons)

Questions to Consider . . . *when working with students as they grapple with the idea of magnitude*

- Are students making decisions about quantity based on the size of the objects in a collection rather than the number of objects in a collection?
- Do students use a systematic way to count a collection?
- What are students paying attention to when they consider how many items are in a collection or the relationship between two or more collections?
- Do students demonstrate an understanding of the quantity or value of a number, not just the ability to read or write a number?

Teacher Sound Bite

"Until I used this probe, I did not understand that some of my students were looking at size of objects rather than number of objects. I am going to make sure that I include many different sized counting objects to help students grasp the idea of magnitude and understand size and quantity are two different ideas that serve different purposes."

Additional References for Research and Teaching Implications

Bay Area Mathematics Task Force (1999), *A Mathematics Source Book for Elementary and Middle School Teachers*, pp. 7–10.

Clements & Sarama (2004), *Engaging Young Children in Mathematics*, p. 94.

NCTM (1993a), *Research Ideas for the Classroom: Early Childhood Mathematics*, pp. 53–68.

NCTM (2000), *Principles and Standards for School Mathematics*, p. 79.

NCTM (2003), *Research Companion to Principles and Standards for School Mathematics*, pp. 78–79.

NRC (2005), *How Students Learn: Mathematics in the Classroom*, p. 272.

Stavy & Tirosh (2000), *How Students (Mis-)Understand Science and Mathematics*, pp. 13–14.

Is One Group More?

Curriculum Topic Study

Related CTS Guide:
Counting

STUDENT RESPONSES TO "IS ONE GROUP MORE?"

Sample Responses: B

Student 1: I think it is B because they are bigger.

Student 2: B is bigger because it looks like more big smiley faces.

Sample Responses: A

Student 3: Group A has more smiley faces because I counted and there are 12 faces.

Student 4: I counted 12 smiley faces in group A and group B has 11. Twelve is more than 11.

VARIATION: DUCKS IN A ROW

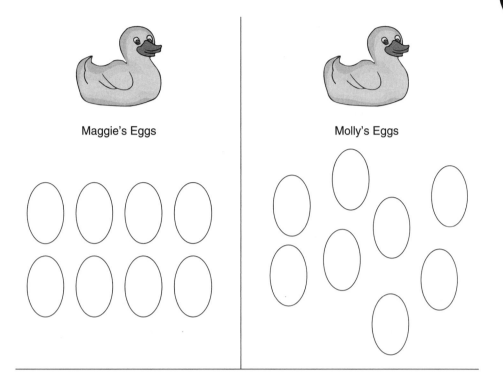

Maggie's Eggs   Molly's Eggs

Circle the sentence that best tells about the number of eggs in each nest.

A. Maggie's has more eggs.

B. Molly's has more eggs.

C. Maggie and Molly have the same amount of eggs.

How did you decide?

_____

_____

_____

_____

BUILDING NUMBERS

Two friends were talking about how to build numbers using blocks. This is what they said:

Samantha: "I think there is only one way to show how to make the number 142 with blocks."

Tucker: "I don't think there's only one way. I think you can show 142 in at least two different ways."

Flat   **Rod**   **Unit**

Which friend do you think is right?

Explain how you know who is correct using as many of the blocks as you like to show your thinking in pictures, words, and/or numbers.

_____

_____

_____

_____

_____

TEACHERS' NOTES: BUILDING NUMBERS

Grade Level for "Building Numbers" Probe

Grades K–2	3–5	6–8	9–12

*Q*uestioning for Student Understanding

What do students understand about our number system and place value?

*U*ncovering Understandings

Building Numbers Content Standard: Number and Operations

*E*xamining Student Work

The distracters may reveal *common errors* regarding place value, such as not considering a number as a whole but rather working with numerals in isolation to compose or decompose numbers.

- *The correct answer is Tucker.* Students who choose to agree with Tucker use the units flexibly to represent multiple configurations of 142. (See Students 3 and 4 in *Student Responses* section.)
- *Students who answered Samantha.* Students who choose to agree with Samantha most likely perceive the digits in isolation related to their place value position and do not consider that 142 could be decomposed in more than one way. (See Students 1 and 2 in *Student Responses* section.)

*S*eeking Links to Cognitive Research

Understanding place value involves building connections between key ideas of place value—such as quantifying sets of objects by grouping by ten and treating the groups as units—and using the structure of the written notation to capture this information about groupings. Different forms of representation for quantities, such as physical materials and written symbols, highlight different aspects of the grouping structure. Building connections between these representations yields a more coherent understanding of place value. (NCTM, 2003, p. 110)

The written place-value system is an efficient system that lets us write large numbers, but it is also abstract and misleading: The numbers in every position look the same. To understand the meaning of the numbers in the various positions, first- and second-grade children need experience with some kind of size visual quantity supports; manipulatives, or drawings that show tens to be collections of 10 ones and show hundreds to be simultaneously 10 tens and 100 ones, and so on. (Clements & Sarama, 2004, p. 125)

Our place value system, which allows us to represent any number with just 10 digits, is not simple for children to understand. Children need to learn to make groups of 10 items and then count those groups as if they were single items. They must learn that digits have different values, depending on their position in numbers. *(Burns, 2000, p. 173)*

Research indicates that students' experiences using physical models to represent hundreds, tens, and ones can be effective if the materials help them think about how to combine quantities and, eventually, how these processes connect with written procedures. (NRC, 2001, p. 96–99)

In grades K–2: It is absolutely essential that students develop a solid understanding of the base-ten numeration system and place-value concepts by the end of Grade 2. *(NCTM, 2000, p. 106)*

In grades 3–5: Students should be computing fluently with whole numbers. Computational fluency refers to having efficient and accurate methods for computing. Students exhibit computational fluency when they demonstrate flexibility in the computational methods they choose, understand and can explain these methods, and produce accurate answers efficiently. The methods that a student uses should be based on mathematical ideas including the structure of the base-ten number system. *(NCTM, 2000, p. 152)*

*T*eaching Implications

To support a deeper understanding for students in elementary school in regard to place value, the following are ideas and questions to consider in conjunction with the research.

Focus Through Instruction

- Students need to learn to make groups of 10 items and then count the groups as a single unit
- Base-ten number knowledge results from an ability to count, to make groupings, and to understand place value at a deeper level than simply naming places
- Practice with the written notation for our number system aligns with how students are building numbers and taking them apart
- Use of physical models encourages students to think about how they are combining quantities
- Use of concrete materials facilitates grouping and ungrouping by tens
- Students should recognize that the word *ten* can represent one unit or ten single units

- Use of a calculator helps to develop and reinforce place value as students interact with the digits and words used along with the visual number formed
- Students can foster understanding of place value through their experiences with combining and comparing numbers as they develop invented strategies for computation
- Students need discussions about their invented strategies to expand both their and others' understanding of place value

Questions to Consider . . . *when working with students as they grapple with these ideas of place value*

- Do students make connections to multiples of 10 and the "bridges" in our number system (i.e., 28, 29, 30, 31, 32), realizing that 10 is a significant unit in our base-ten number system?
- Do they refer to the digits in the tens and hundreds places as a single digit, or do they keep their value whole when they compose and decompose numbers?
- Are students able to confidently show how to "build a number" in more than one way?
- Can students generalize the pattern of tens to count and build numbers over 100?
- Are students thinking of a number as a group of symbols side by side rather than as an entity?

Teacher Sound Bite

"I've noticed that my students are more likely to think about the whole instead of separate digits when they have access to manipulatives. As they experiment with number problems and build some initial strategies for combining and comparing numbers, they are composing and decomposing numbers with emphasis on place value."

Additional References for Research and Teaching Implications

Burns (2000), *About Teaching Mathematics: A K–8 Resource*, p. 173.
Clements & Sarama (2004), *Engaging Young Children in Mathematics*, p. 125.
NCTM (1993a), *Research Ideas for the Classroom: Early Childhood Mathematics*, pp. 53–68.
NCTM (2000), *Principles and Standards for School Mathematics*, pp. 106, 152.
NCTM (2003), *Research Companion to Principles and Standards for School Mathematics*, pp. 78–79.
NRC (2001), *Adding It Up: Helping Children Learn Mathematics*, pp. 96–99.
Wearne & Hiebert (2001), *Putting Research Into Practice in the Elementary Grades*, p. 110.

Building Numbers
Curriculum Topic Study
Related CTS Guide: Place Value

STUDENT RESPONSES TO "BUILDING NUMBERS"

Sample Responses: Samantha

Student 1: I know that it only takes 1 flat, 4 tens, and 2 ones to make this number because those are the names of the numbers, like 1 hundred, forty is 4 tens, and 2 ones.

Student 2: I agree with Samantha because it is obvious that there is only 1 hundred, 4 tens, and 2 ones.

Sample Responses: Tucker

Student 3: I think Tucker is right because besides just 1 flat, 4 rods, and 2 units, you could use 142 units. All numbers can be made out of ones, just some are a lot of ones.

Student 4: Tucker is right because I can make 142 with 1 hundred, 4 tens, and 2 ones, or 14 tens and 2 ones, or 142 ones. There are three ways to show this number.

ARE THEY EQUAL?

Use *mental math* to decide if the number sentence pairs are equal or not equal.

Explain your thinking.

A.	
24 + 45	45 + 24

_____

_____

_____

_____

_____

_____

B.	
24 – 13	13 – 24

_____

_____

_____

_____

_____

_____

C.	
34 + 76	36 + 74

_____

_____

_____

_____

_____

_____

D.	
45 – 32	42 – 35

_____

_____

_____

_____

_____

_____

TEACHERS' NOTES: ARE THEY EQUAL?

Grade Level for "Are They Equal?" Probe

Grades K–2	3–5	6–8	9–12

*Q*uestioning for Student Understanding

What do students understand about the commutative and associative properties as they relate to the numbers used in addition and subtraction equations?

*U*ncovering Understandings

Are They Equal? Content Standard: Number and Operations
Variation: Are They Equal? (appropriate for Grades 6 through 8 using decimals)

*E*xamining Student Work:

The distracters may reveal *overgeneralizations* as students apply properties without considering the operation implied by the symbol being used.

- *The equal pairs are A and C.* Students who indicate that the equations in A and C are equal apply the ideas of the commutative and associative property effectively to make their decisions. (See Students 5 and 6 in *Student Responses* section.)
- *Students who answered A, C, and D.* Students who indicate that the equations in A, C, and D are equal can apply the commutative and associative properties with addition; however, because they thought the D equations were equal, they do not seem to consider the idea of *constant difference.* (See Students 1 and 2 in *Student Responses* section.)
- *Students who answered A.* Students who that the equations in A were the only equal pair most often look at the change in the numbers used, specifically referencing the digit in the ones place. Their rationale for inequality is that by changing the digits and not just switching the order of the numbers (as in A), the number sentences were not equal. (See Students 3 and 4 in *Student Responses* section.)

*S*eeking Links to Cognitive Research

To really understand addition and subtraction, we must understand how they are connected. We must also have a generalized model of the operation, one that can be used as a tool to think with no matter what the context (e.g., understanding how removal and comparison contexts can both be solved by subtraction on a number line). By modeling addition and subtraction situations and then generalizing across these situations, children are able to understand and represent the operations of addition and subtraction. *(Fosnot & Dolk, 2001, p. 97)*

Calculating with number sense means that one must look at the numbers first and then decide on a strategy that is fitting—and efficient. Children who learn to think, rather than to apply the same procedures by rote regardless of the numbers, will be empowered. (Fosnot & Dolk, 2001, p. 97)

In developing the meaning of addition and subtraction with whole numbers, students should also encounter the properties of operations, such as commutativity and associativity of addition. Although some students discover and use properties of operations naturally, teachers can bring these properties to the forefront through class discussions. (NCTM, 2000, pp. 83–84)

Addition is more than just "putting together," and subtraction is more than "take-away." Addition and subtraction are the appropriate operations for a variety of situations. Recognizing these situations can lead to success with word problems and problem solving, and can aid in the learning of number facts. (Bay Area Mathematics Task Force, 1999, pp. 14–26)

In grades K–2, students develop the meaning of operations as they encounter situations in which the same number appears in different contexts. Although different students may initially use quite different ways of thinking to solve problems, teachers should help students recognize that solving one kind of problem is related to solving another kind. Recognizing the inverse relationship between addition and subtraction can allow students to be flexible in using strategies to solve problems. *(NCTM, 2000. p. 83)*

In grades 3–5, a major goal is the development of computational fluency with whole numbers. Fluency refers to having efficient, accurate, and generalizable methods (algorithms) for computing that are based on well-understood properties and number relationships. Some of these methods are performed mentally, and others are carried out using paper and pencil to facilitate the recording of thinking. (NCTM. 2000, p. 144)

*T*eaching Implications

To support a deeper understanding for students in elementary school in regard to computation, specifically with understanding the associative and commutative properties, the following are ideas and questions to consider in conjunction with the research.

Focus Through Instruction

- Help students understand that addition and subtraction are inverse operations
- Have students orally narrate their actions during early addition and subtraction experiences to reinforce the action
- Make connections between addition and subtraction facts to support the idea of inverse operations
- Support fact building through student-invented strategies
- Point out to students that the commutative property in addition cannot be generalized to subtraction as 5 + 3 is the same as 3 + 5, whereas 5 − 3 is not the same as 3 − 5
- Make sure to support student recognition of the relationships between numbers used in problems

Questions to Consider . . . *when working with students as they grapple with the idea of commutative and associative properties*

- As students work with addition situations, what do they do with the order of the addends?
- Do students demonstrate an understanding of subtraction as the difference between two numbers?
- When presented with story problems what are ways students construct their number sentences?
- Do they consider the relationship of the numbers in the problem as a strategy to solve the problem?

Teacher Sound Bite

"When I looked at my students' responses, I was surprised that half of my students chose C as not equal and D as equal. I made assumptions about their understanding of the properties. Clearly, there was some clarifying that needed to take place as we were working with all four operations now. Instead of pointing out the properties in isolation of a context, I decided to use what I knew from the probes to have my students use a strategy of creating examples and nonexamples of the properties from their own work as we continued to work with addition and subtraction to specifically reference in our class discussions."

Additional References for Research and Teaching Implications

Bay Area Mathematics Task Force (1999), *A Mathematics Source Book for Elementary and Middle School Teachers*, pp. 14–26.

Fosnot & Dolk (2001), *Young Mathematicians at Work: Constructing Number Sense, Addition and Subtraction*, p. 97.

NCTM (1993a), *Research Ideas for the Classroom: Early Childhood Mathematics*, pp. 72–99.

NCTM (2000), *Principles and Standards for School Mathematics*, pp. 83–84, 144.

NRC (2001), *Adding It Up: Helping Children Learn Mathematics*, pp. 181–218.

Are They Equal?
Curriculum Topic Study
Related CTS Guide: Addition and Subtraction

STUDENT RESPONSES TO "ARE THEY EQUAL?"

Sample Responses: ACD

Student 1: A is a turnaround. B is 24–13 = 11, and 13–24 is below zero. In C, the two numbers are the same because in one it's 34 and 76 and in the other the 70 has a 4 and the 30 has the 6. D is a turnaround of ones. The 30 has a 5, and the 40 has the 2.

Student 2: A is the same since both problems are adding the same numbers. B is not equal since they're both subtracting 13 from a different number. C and D are equal since the problems both have the same amount of tens and the same amount of ones; the answer is equal.

Sample Responses: A

Student 3: A is the same math problems except switched. B is two different math problems. C is two different problems, and D is two different problems.

Student 4: If the numbers are switched around and have the same sign, they would be equal.

Sample Responses: AC

Student 5: In A, they switched sides and add up to the same. In B, 13–24 would be a negative number, and 24–13 would not be negative. C is equal because the 6 on 76 switches to the 4 on 74. The 4 on 34 switches with the 6 in 36. D is not equal because 45–32 = 13 and 42–35 = 7, so they are different.

Student 6: I know that with addition you can change which number comes first. With subtraction you can't do that.

Probe
3a

VARIATION: ARE THEY EQUAL?

Use *mental math* to decide if the number sentence pairs are equal or not equal.
Explain how you made your decision.

A.

22.4 + 14.5   14.5 + 22.4

_____
_____
_____
_____
_____

B.

53.4 – 21.3   21.3 – 53.4

_____
_____
_____
_____
_____

C.

53.4 + 17.6   53.6 + 17.4

_____
_____
_____
_____
_____
_____

D.

34.5 – 43.2   34.2 – 43.5

_____
_____
_____
_____
_____
_____

FRACTIONAL PARTS

What fraction of the circle does B represent?

Answer: _____

Explain your thinking.

_____

_____

_____

_____

_____

_____

_____

TEACHERS' NOTES: FRACTIONAL PARTS

Grade Level for "Fractional Parts" Probe

Grades K–2	3–5	6–8	9–12

*Q*uestioning for Student Understanding

What do students understand about part-whole relationships in identifying fractional parts?

*U*ncovering Understandings

Fractional Parts Content Standard: Number and Operations
Variation: Fraction ID

*E*xamining Student Work

The distracters may reveal *overgeneralizations* regarding application of whole number properties to working with fractions.

- *The correct answer is 1/4.* Students who answer 1/4 most likely consider the size of B as it relates to the whole circle. They are using knowledge of part-whole relationships. (See Students 5 and 6 in *Student Responses* section.)
- *Students who answered 1/5.* Students who answer 1/5 considered the total number of pieces of the circle without relating to the size of the pieces within the circle. They most likely see all pieces as the total, much as in whole numbers, without considering the varying size of pieces in the circle. (See Students 1 and 2 in *Student Responses* section.)
- *Students who answered "Other."* Students who chose other fractions or whole numbers displayed difficulty defining a part-whole relationship. (See Students 3 and 4 in *Student Responses* section.)

*S*eeking Links to Cognitive Research

Of all the ways in which rational numbers can be interpreted and used, the most basic is the simplest—rational numbers are numbers. The fact is so fundamental that [it] is easily overlooked. A rational number like 3/4 is a single entity just as the number 5 is a single entity. Each rational number holds a unique place (or is a unique length) on the number line. Further, the way common fractions are written (e.g., 3/4) does not help students see a rational number as a distinct number. Research has verified what many teachers have observed, that students continue to use properties they learned from operating with whole numbers even though many whole number properties do not apply to rational numbers. With common fractions, for example, students may reason that 1/8 is larger than 1/7 because 8 is larger than 7. Or they may believe that 3/4 equals 4/5 because in both fractions the difference between numerator and denominator is 1. (NRC, 2001, p. 235)

One of the primary characteristics of students' informal knowledge of fractions is that students' informal solutions involve separating units into parts and dealing with each part as though it represents a whole number, as opposed to dealing with each part as a fraction (Mack 1990). For example, consider the following problem: If you have 5/6 of a cake and I eat 2/6 of the cake, how much of the cake do you have left? Students often refer to the fractions in the problem in terms of the "number or pieces" (e.g., five pieces or five pieces of six). However, the use of fraction names (e.g., five-sixths) refers to the fractions as specific parts of a whole. (NCTM, 2002, p. 137)

Fractions make it possible to represent numbers between whole numbers. Fractions express numbers as an indicated division of two whole numbers. A fraction bar indicates the division. Some of the main ways that fractions are used in elementary school are as part of the whole, as quotient representations of ratios, as measures, as individual numbers on a number line, and in computation. (Bay Area Mathematics Task Force, 1999, p. 59)

In grades K–2, in addition to work with whole numbers, young students should also have some experience with simple fractions through connections to everyday situations and meaningful problems, starting with the common fractions expressed in the language they bring to the classroom, such as "half." At this level it is more important for students to recognize when things are divided into equal parts than to focus on fraction notation. (NCTM, 2000, p. 82)

In grades 3–5, students should build their understanding of fractions as parts of a whole and as division. They will need to see and explore a variety of models of fractions, focusing primarily on familiar fractions such as halves, thirds, fourths, fifths, sixths, eighths, and tenths. By using an area model in which part of a region is shaded, students can see how fractions are related to a unit whole, compare fractional parts of a whole, and find equivalent fractions. They should develop strategies for ordering and comparing fractions, often using benchmarks such as 1/2 and 1. (NCTM, 2000, p. 150)

In grades 6–8, students should deepen their understanding of *fractions*, decimals, percents, and integers, and they should become proficient in using them to solve problems. Students should have learned to generate and recognize equivalent forms of *fractions*, decimals, and percents, at least in some simple cases in grades 3–5. (NCTM, 2000, p. 215)

Teaching Implications

To support a deeper understanding for students in elementary school in regard to fractions, specifically with identifying the size of fractional parts, the following are ideas and questions to consider in conjunction with the research.

Focus Through Instruction

- Students should make comparisons between numbers by using their understanding of equivalence
- Students need experience considering that fractions have precise locations and values in our number system
- Students should see various meanings and models of fractions; how they are related to each other and to the unit whole and how they are represented
- Models such as the number line and thermometer allow students to consider numbers less than zero
- Use of an area model allows students to "see" the part-to-whole relationship
- Students should develop strategies for ordering and comparing fractions
- Students should learn to use benchmarks, for example, 1/2 and 1, to compare size
- Students should become familiar with equivalent fractions

Questions to Consider . . . *when working with students as they grapple with the ideas of fractions*

- Do students use what they know about whole numbers when working with fractions?
- Can students make connections about relative size of fractions in relation to whole numbers?
- Do students use their knowledge of division in working with fractions?
- Are students using models to represent their thinking as proof of equivalence and to demonstrate their understanding of fractions?

Teacher Sound Bite

"I believed that my Grade 5 students would have no difficulty correctly identifying B as 1/4. I was disappointed in my assumption when I realized that more than half of my students chose 1/5 along with some 2/6, 1/3, and various nonfraction representations. Giving this probe and seeing my students' explanations, I was able also to see that some students who correctly said 1/4 did not have solid reasoning for their decision, and this prompted me to design some instruction related to the findings of the probe."

Additional References for Research and Teaching Implications

Bay Area Mathematics Task Force (1999), *A Mathematics Source Book for Elementary and Middle School Teachers*, pp. 59–70.

NCTM (1993a), *Research Ideas for the Classroom: Early Childhood Mathematics*, pp. 11–15.

NCTM (2000), *Principles and Standards for School Mathematics*, pp. 82, 150, 215.

NRC (2001), *Adding It Up: Helping Children Learn Mathematics*, p. 235.

Wearne & Hiebert (2001), *Putting Research Into Practice in the Elementary Grades*, p. 137.

Fractional Parts
Curriculum Topic Study
Related CTS Guide: Fractions

STUDENT RESPONSES TO "FRACTIONAL PARTS"

Sample Responses: 1/5

Student 1: There are five blocks, and B is one out of the five so you make a line and put five on the bottom and one on the top.

Student 2: There are five sections, and B represents one section filled in so therefore it is 1/5.

Sample Responses: Other

Student 3: I think it is one and a half fifth because it takes up that much of the circle.

Student 4: 1/2 out of 5/5 because B and C are a little bit bigger than A, D, and E.

Sample Responses: 1/4

Student 5: 1/4 because if you split the circle into 4 groups B is 25% of the whole and 1/4 equals 25%.

Student 6: B is 1/4 of the circle because half of a half of the circle is B.

VARIATION: FRACTION ID

Circle the items that show ¼ of the whole.

a)	b)
c)	d)
e)	f)
g)	h)
i)	j)

How did you decide if the item showed ¼ of the whole?

_____

_____

_____

_____

COMPARING DECIMALS

In each pair of numbers, circle the one that is larger.

A.	
0.175	.2

B.	
3.642	3.35

C.	
0.00753	.1075

Explain your process for deciding which numbers were larger:

_____

_____

_____

_____

_____

_____

_____

_____

_____

TEACHERS' NOTES: COMPARING DECIMALS

Grade Level for "Comparing Decimals" Probe

Grades K–2	3–5	6–8	9–12

Questioning for Student Understanding

Do students consider place value when comparing the size of decimals?

Uncovering Understandings

Comparing Decimals Content Standard: Number and Operations
Variation: Comparing Decimals II

Examining Student Work

The distracters may reveal a lack of *conceptual* understanding of the size of a decimal and an *overgeneralization* from prior work with whole numbers or fractions.

- *The correct answers are (A) 0.2, (B) 3.642, and (C) 0.1075.* The majority of students who solve this correctly use the process of comparing digits in each place. (See Students 1 and 2 in *Student Responses* section.)
- *Distracter (A) 0.175, (B) 3.642, and (C) 0.00753.* Students choosing this combination often use the reasoning similar to "more digits to the right of the decimal point." (See Students 3 and 4 in *Student Responses* section.)
- *Distracter (A) 0.175, (B) 3.642, and (C) 0.1075.* Students choosing this combination often refer to the numbers to the right of the decimal point as whole numbers, such as 175 is larger than 2, 1075 is larger than 753. (See Student 5 in *Student Responses* section.)
- *Distracter (A) 0.175, (B) 3.642, and (C) 0.00753.* Students choosing this combination often use the reasoning "the more digits the smaller the number." (See Student 6 in *Student Responses* section.)

Seeking Links to Cognitive Research

Many upper elementary and middle-school students cannot successfully compare decimal numbers. They may *overgeneralize* the features of the whole number system and apply a "more digits makes bigger" rule. (AAAS, 1993, p. 359)

In a study of 113 fourth graders, the children who treated decimal fractions as they would treat whole numbers believed the number with more decimal places is the greatest number. The children who treated decimal fractions as they would treat common fractions believed that the number with more decimal places is the lesser number. Both of these overgeneralized ideas can, at times, generate a correct response. (NCTM, 1993a, p. 243)

*T*eaching Implications

To support a deeper understanding for students in middle school in regard to decimals, the following are ideas and questions to consider in conjunction with the research.

Focus Through Instruction

- Offer students models as concrete representations of abstract ideas
- Use models such as base-ten blocks, number lines, and 10×10 grid paper to represent and study decimal numbers
- Use benchmarks in judging the size of decimals
- Provide a context (such as money) when working with decimals
- Construct equivalent forms of decimals to help establish an understanding of place value

Questions to Consider . . . *when working with students as they grapple with the comparison of decimals*

- Are students able to judge the size of a decimal by using a benchmark?
- Are students able to use a model to correctly compare decimals?
- Are students able to decompose/partition decimals in a number of ways?
- Are students able to place decimals appropriately on a number line?

Teacher Sound Bite

"By looking at student work, I saw that the traditionally taught procedure (lining up the numbers and comparing individual place values to compare decimals) did not help all of my students understand the size of each of the numbers. Many students lacked a conceptual understanding, which I tried to establish by using manipulatives and grid paper. This strategy helps students visualize the size of the decimals."

Additional References for Research and Teaching Implications

NCTM (1993a), *Research Ideas for the Classroom: Early Childhood Mathematics*, pp. 242–245.

NCTM (2000), *Principles and Standards for School Mathematics*, pp. 32–33, 150, 214–221.

NRC (2001), *Adding It Up: Helping Children Learn Mathematics*, pp. 246–247.

Stavy & Tirosh (2000), *How Students (Mis-)Understand Science and Mathematics*, pp. 1–2, 31.

> **Comparing Decimals**
>
> *Curriculum Topic Study*
>
> Related CTS Guide:
> Decimals and Division

STUDENT RESPONSES TO "COMPARING DECIMALS"

Sample Responses: (A) 0.2, (B) 3.642, and (C) 0.1075

Student 1: I added zeros if I had to so they each have the same number of digits. Then I look at what place it was in to determine the bigger number.

Student 2: I looked at the numbers in the ones place first. Then the tenths place, then the hundredth digit, and so on.

Sample Responses: (A) 0.175, (B) 3.642, and (C) 0.00753

Student 3: I just thought back to what I learned about decimal places.

Student 4: I counted the numbers after the decimal.

Sample Response: (A) 0.175, (B) 3.642, and (C) 0.1075

Student 5: 175 thousands is bigger than 2 tens and I used the same process for the rest.

Sample Response: (A) 0.175, (B) 3.642, and (C) 0.00753

Student 6: As the numbers after the decimal get longer, the number gets smaller.

VARIATION: **COMPARING DECIMALS II**

Probe
5a

The digits in the following numbers are hidden.

A. 4. [] [] [] []   B. 4. [] []

What is true about the numbers?

Circle the true statement about the numbers.

1. A is larger than B

2. B is larger than A

3. Not enough information to decide

Explain your thought process.

_____

_____

_____

_____

_____

_____

_____

_____

_____

COMPARING FRACTIONS

Decide which fraction is bigger in each box, and describe how you made your decision for each pair.

1.

A. $\dfrac{5}{6}$ B. $\dfrac{5}{9}$

_____
_____
_____
_____
_____

2.

A. $\dfrac{2}{3}$ B. $\dfrac{2}{4}$

_____
_____
_____
_____
_____
_____

3.

A. $\dfrac{1}{5}$ B. $\dfrac{2}{10}$

_____
_____
_____
_____
_____
_____

4.

A. $\dfrac{2}{3}$ B. $\dfrac{2}{5}$

_____
_____
_____
_____
_____

TEACHERS' NOTES: COMPARING FRACTIONS

Grade Level for "Comparing Fractions" Probe

Grades K–2	3–5	6–8	9–12

Questioning for Student Understanding

What do students understand about part-whole relationships when comparing fractions?

Uncovering Understandings

Comparing Fractions Content Standard: Number and Operations

Examining Student Work

The distracters may reveal *common errors* regarding students' understanding of part-whole relationships as they relate to comparing fractions to decide which is bigger. Errors occur when students apply their knowledge of whole numbers to those of fractions.

- *The correct answers are 5/6, 2/3, the same, 2/3.* These responses demonstrate an understanding the relationship between the two fractions, considering the part-whole relationship rather than just concluding that a larger denominator means a larger fraction. (See Students 5 and 6 in *Student Responses* section.)
- *Students who answered B for All.* Students who choose B for all responses, signifying that B is the bigger fraction in each pair, are applying the whole number property of larger means bigger. They look primarily at the denominator to determine relative size. They are incorrectly applying the properties of working with whole numbers to fractions. (See Students 1 and 2 in *Student Responses* section.)
- *Students who answered 5/6, 2/3, 1/5, 2/3.* Students who choose 5/6, 2/3, 1/5, and 2/3 as the bigger fraction in each pair are using similar thinking in identifying the larger fraction. When deciding between 1/5 and 2/10, for example, students continue to apply the idea that the smaller denominator is the bigger fraction without considering the relationship between the numerator and denominator. (See Students 3 and 4 in *Student Responses* section.)

Seeking Links to Cognitive Research

Many conventional curricula introduce rational numbers as common fractions that stand for part of a whole, but little attention is given to the whole from which the rational number extracts its meaning. For example, many students first see a fraction as, say, 3/4 of a pizza. In this interpretation, the amount of pizza is determined by the fractional part (3/4) *and* by the size of the pizza. Hence, three fourths of a medium pizza is not the same amount of pizza as three fourths of a large pizza, although it may be the same number of pieces. Lack of attention to the nature of the unit or whole may explain many of the misconceptions that students exhibit. (NRC, 2001, p. 237)

A cursory look at some typical student misunderstandings illuminates the kinds of problems students have with rational numbers. The culprit appears to be the continued use of whole-number reasoning in situations where it does not apply. Faulty whole-number reasoning causes students to maintain, for example, that the fraction 1/8 is larger than 1/6 because, as they say, "8 is a bigger number than 6." Not surprisingly, students struggle with calculations as well. When asked to find the sum of 1/2 and 1/3, the majority of fourth and sixth graders give the same answer 2/5. Even after a number of years working with fractions, some eighth graders make the same error, illustrating that they still mistakenly count the numerator and denominator as separate numbers to find a sum. Clearly whole-number reasoning is very resilient. (NRC, 2005, p. 310)

Providing students with many experiences in partitioning quantities into equal parts using concrete models, pictures, and meaningful contexts can help them create meaning for fraction notations. Introducing the standard notation for common fractions and decimals must be done with care, ensuring that students are able to connect the meanings already developed for the numbers with the symbols that represent them. (NRC, 2001, p. 236)

In grades 3–5, students should build their understanding of fractions as parts of a whole and as division. They will need to see and explore a variety of models of fractions, focusing primarily on familiar fractions such as halves, thirds, fourths, fifths, sixths, eighths, and tenths. By using an area model in which part of a region is shaded, students can see how fractions are related to a unit whole, compare fractional parts of a whole, and find equivalent fractions. They should develop strategies for ordering and comparing fractions, often using benchmarks such as 1/2 and 1. (NCTM, 2000, p. 150)

A significant amount of instructional time should be devoted to rational numbers in grades 3–5. The focus should be on developing students' conceptual understanding of fractions and decimals—what they are, how they are represented, and how they are related to whole numbers—rather than on developing computational fluency with rational numbers. Fluency in rational-number computation will be a major focus in grades 6–8. (NCTM, 2000, p. 152)

In grades 6–8, students should extend their experiences to tasks in which they order or compare fractions, which many students find difficult. For example, fewer than one-third of the thirteen-year-old U.S. students tested by the NAEP in 1988 correctly chose the largest number from 3/4, 9/16, 5/8, and 2/3. Students' difficulties with comparison of fractions have also been documented in more recent NAEP administrations. (NCTM, 2000, p. 216)

*T*eaching Implications

To support a deeper understanding for students in elementary school in regard to fractions, specifically with comparing fractions, the following are ideas and questions to consider in conjunction with the research.

Focus Through Instruction

- Develop students' ability to understand the many meanings and representations of fractions before teaching rules and procedures for calculating with fractions
- Show students how to use models based on area, sets of things, and linear measurement
- Use different models to help with recognition and solution of different problem situations
- Begin with the concept of a whole that is a single unit that can be divided up into equal-sized parts
- Develop understanding of uses of equivalent fractions through real-life problems
- Use number lines and rulers to emphasize units and equal subdivisions
- Focus attention on the use of equal-size wholes, equal-size parts, and equivalent fractions during informal experiences comparing fractional quantities

Questions to Consider . . . *when working with students as they grapple with the idea of comparing fractions*

- Do students use accurate vocabulary when naming fractions?
- Are they able to support their comparisons using models?
- Do students demonstrate an understanding of what the parts of a fraction mean?
- What do students pay attention to as they make decisions about whether fractions are greater than, less than, or equivalent?

Teacher Sound Bite

"Prior to using this probe with my Grade 6 students, I was pretty confident in their understanding of fractions to tenths. They had previous experience in elementary school and could identify simple fractions and put them in order using fraction tracks. What surprised me was the results of this probe in that many of my students, without the structure of the graphic organizer, were unable to distinguish the bigger fraction successfully. Based on this information, I have begun to add many models, languages, and experiences for my students, and this is better enabling them to think about fractions as rational numbers."

Additional References for Research and Teaching Implications

Comparing Fractions
Curriculum Topic Study
Related CTS Guide: Fractions

Bay Area Mathematics Task Force (1999), *A Mathematics Source Book for Elementary and Middle School Teachers*, pp. 59–70.

NCTM (2000), *Principles and Standards for School Mathematics*, pp. 150, 152, 216.

NRC (2001), *Adding It Up: Helping Children Learn Mathematics*, pp. 261–283, 237.

NRC (2005), *How Students Learn: Mathematics in the Classroom*, p. 310.

STUDENT RESPONSES TO "COMPARING FRACTIONS"

Sample Responses: B for All

Student 1: I thought the bigger numbers would be bigger.

Student 2: I looked at the top number in box. In 1, it was the same 5, but the bottom number 9 was bigger, so 5/9 is bigger. Box 4 was the same because 5 is bigger than 3. In Box 2, B is bigger because the 3 is on top and a 2 on the other one. And the same for Box 3, 2 is bigger than 1.

Sample Responses: 5/6, 2/3, 1/5, 2/3

Student 3: 1/5 is bigger because in the third one, for example, 1/5 is just bigger. You would have to add 4 to get 5/5, and with 2/10, you would have to add 8 to get 10/10.

Student 4: The smaller the denominator, the bigger the fraction, so 5 is bigger than 10.

Sample Responses: 5/6, 2/3, the same, 2/3

Student 5: I go by if the bottom is bigger, then the fraction is smaller because it means in 5/9 that there are 9 pieces of 1, and 5/6 there are 6 pieces out of the same 1 so 5/6 is bigger.

Student 6: It matters by size—if the number on the bottom is higher, then it is a smaller fraction.

ORDER OF OPERAT

Three students were asked to solve the following expression:

$$46 - 30 \div 2 \times 3 + 6.$$

Which solution do you think is correct?

Laura's Solution:	*Brian's Solution:*	*Kelly's Solution:*
$46 - 30 \div 2 \times 3 + 6$	$46 - 30 \div 2 \times 3 + 6$	$46 - 30 \div 2 \times 3 + 6$
$16 \div 2 \times 3 + 6$	$46 - 30 \div 6 + 6$	$46 - 15 \times 3 + 6$
$8 \times 3 + 6$	$46 - 5 + 6$	$46 - 45 + 6$
$24 + 6$	$41 + 6$	$1 + 6$
30	47	7

Explain why you agree with the solution you selected.

_____

_____

_____

_____

_____

_____

_____

_____

TEACHERS' NOTES: ORDER OF OPERATIONS

Grade Level for "Order of Operations" Probe

Grades K–2	3–5	6–8	9–12

*Q*uestioning for Student Understanding

When simplifying expressions, do students follow the rules for the order of operations?

*U*ncovering Understandings

Order of Operations Content Standard: Number and Operations
Variation: Order of Operations II (using the contrasting opposing views format)

*E*xamining Student Work

The distracters may reveal students' lack of *procedural* understanding of the rules for the order of operations.

- *The correct response is Kelly's solution.* Kelly uses the rules for the order of operations (commonly referred to as PEMDAS) while working from left to right. She divides 30 by 2 before multiplying 2 by 3. (See Student 1 in *Student Responses* section.)
- *Distracter A (Laura's solution).* Students who choose Laura's solution generally work from left to right without using the rules for the order of operations. (See Students 2 and 3 in *Student Responses* section.)
- *Distracter B (Brian's solution).* Students who choose Brian's solution typically use the rules for the order of operations without working from left to right. They compute multiplication before division and addition before subtraction. (See Students 4, 5, and 6 in *Student Responses* section.)

*S*eeking Links to Cognitive Research

Developing fluency requires a balance and connection between conceptual understanding and computational proficiency. Computational methods that are over-practiced without understanding are often forgotten or remembered incorrectly (Hiebert, 1999; Kamii, Lewis, and Livingston 1993; Hiebert and Lindquist 1990). (NCTM, 2000, p. 35)

To sixth graders, [the rules for the order of operations] must appear random and therefore meaningless, and the meaninglessness of it all gives rise to the infamous Please Excuse My Dear Aunt Sally mnemonic device. Another universally accepted algebraic "rule" is: (A) exponents first, then multiplications, then additions. The rule of "multiplications before additions" may sound simple, but these three words contain more than meets the eye. Because we are in the realm of algebra, "division by a (nonzero) number c" is the same as "multiplication by 1/c." Moreover, "minus c" is the same as "plus (-c). Therefore if one rewrites what is in statement (A) above in the language of arithmetic, then one would have to expand it to: (B) exponents first, then multiplications and divisions, then additions and subtractions. Except for the stipulation about performing the operations "from left to right," (B) is seen to be exactly the same as the Rules for the Order of Operations. (http://math .berkeley.edu/~wu/order3.pdf)

*T*eaching Implications

To support a deeper understanding for students in middle school in regard to simplifying expressions using orders of operations, the following are ideas and questions to consider in conjunction with the research.

Focus Through Instruction

- Students misapply rules they have learned as isolated mathematical procedures
- Learning facts and algorithms needs to be a building stone of the active mathematical knowledge of students
- In classrooms in which the focus is teaching for understanding, students develop a wider range of effective methods, whereas in classrooms in which rote learning methods are used, students' inventiveness often generates many different kinds of errors, most of which are partially correct methods created by a particular misunderstanding

Questions to Consider . . . *when working with students as they grapple with the idea of simplifying expressions using orders of operations*

- If students use PEMDAS as a mnemonic, do they understand multiplication is not always calculated prior to division and the same for addition and subtraction?
- Are students able to create a contextual problem that requires use of a specific order of operation?
- Do students understand order of operations as a convention?

Teacher Sound Bite

"This probe helped me to see why my students were having difficulties with simplifying expressions. Many of them did not work from left to right when applying the order of operations. I will need to make sure we work on a better conceptual understanding of operations with numbers before we move to a procedural understanding."

Additional References for Research and Teaching Implications

AAAS (1993), *Benchmarks for Science Literacy*, pp. 210, 213, 288–289.

NCTM (1993c), *Research Ideas for the Classroom: Middle Grades Mathematics*, pp. 112–114.

NCTM (2000), *Principles and Standards for School Mathematics*, pp. 32–33, 35, (Grades 3–5) pp. 148, 152–156, (Grades 6–8) pp. 214, 220–221.

NCTM (2003), *A Research Companion to Principles and Standards for School Mathematics*, pp. 71–72, 87–89, 114, 120–121.

> **Order of Operations**
>
> *Curriculum Topic Study*
>
> Related CTS Guide:
> Properties of Operations

STUDENT RESPONSES TO "ORDER OF OPERATIONS"

Sample Response: Kelly

Student 1: I used the order of operations as it states in the name of the problem. There were no parentheses or exponents so all I had to worry about was the MDAS in PEMDAS. I know that multiplication and/or division comes first depending on which is more toward the left. Then I finished it off by doing the addition and/or subtracting. My work and answer was the same as Kelly's.

Sample Responses: Laura

Student 2: I subtracted 46 by 30, divided it by 2, times it by 3, and added 6. (Laura's solution was circled.)

Student 3: Laura is correct. My explanation is that Brian started with 2 × 3, and the problem does not have parenthesis. Kelly is also wrong because she started with 30 ÷ 2, and the problem does not read that way.

Sample Responses: Brian

Student 4: PEMDAS . . . I agree with Brian because he is the only person who multiplied first and then divided next, then subtracted, and then added. After Brian added, he got 47 for his answer.

Student 5: I agree with Brian's solution because the others didn't do order of operations. Multiplication would be the first thing to do here because there are no parentheses or exponents.

Sample Response: Other

Student 6: I think none of them are correct because (1) none of them have the right answer and (2) they don't follow order of operations: 2 × 3 = 6, 30 ÷ 6 = 5, 5 + 6 = 11, 46 − 11 = 35.

VARIATION: ORDER OF OPERATIONS II

Two students were asked to compute $46 - 30 \div 2 \times 3 + 6$

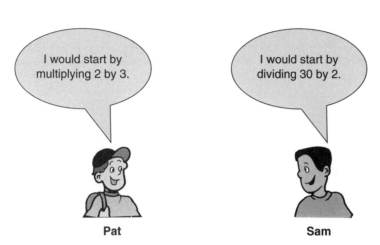

I would start by multiplying 2 by 3.

Pat

I would start by dividing 30 by 2.

Sam

Who do you agree with? Explain your choice.

_____

_____

_____

_____

_____

_____

_____

_____

WHICH IS BIGGER?

Use *mental math* to decide which problem has the bigger answer or if they are the same. Describe how you made your decision in each case.

1.

A. 34 × 21

B. 34 + 21

_____
_____
_____
_____
_____
_____

2.

A. 34 + .21

B. 34 × .21

_____
_____
_____
_____
_____
_____

3.

A. 21 + 3.4

B. 21 × 3.4

_____
_____
_____
_____
_____
_____

4.

A. .21 × .34

B. .21 + .34

_____
_____
_____
_____
_____
_____

TEACHERS' NOTES: WHICH IS BIGGER?

Grade Level for "Which Is Bigger?" Probe

Grades K–2	3–5	6–8	9–12

Questioning for Student Understanding

Do students understand the effect of multiplication and division on different numbers?

Uncovering Understandings

Which Is Bigger? Content Standard: Number and Operations
Variations: Multiplication Makes Bigger, Which Is Bigger ? II

Examining Student Work

The distracters may reveal the common misconception regarding the operations of multiplication and division: that "multiplication makes bigger" and "division makes smaller." These misconceptions result from *overgeneralizing* the effect of the operations on whole numbers.

- *The correct answers are 1A, 2A, 3B, 4B.* The fours sets are designed to incorporate whole numbers (34, 21), whole numbers with a number less than 1 (34, .21), whole numbers with a decimal greater than one (21, 3.4), and both numbers less than one (.21, .34). In the field test of this probe, very few students were able to choose all four correct answers although the majority did choose one correctly.
- *Choices 1A, 2B, 3B, 4A.* These answers are chosen by students who *overgeneralize,* "multiplication always makes bigger" (See Students 1 through 7 in *Student Responses* section.)
- *Choices 1A, 2A, 3A, 4A.* Some students choose A as bigger for each of the paired sets. The most common explanation given was the *overgeneralization,* "multiplication always makes bigger." Additional interviews in the field-testing of this probe revealed the common error of not paying attention to the order of the problems given (they looked at the problem quickly and assumed the multiplication were As).
- *Choices A and B are equal.* The students who make this choice typically do so on set 3 and 4. Additional field-test interviews show that these students make a procedural error while computing. (See Student 8 in *Student Responses* section.)

Seeking Links to Cognitive Research

Multiplying and dividing fractions and decimals can be challenging for many students because of problems that are primarily conceptual rather than procedural. From their experience with whole numbers, many students appear to develop a belief that "multiplication makes bigger and division make smaller." (NCTM, 2000, p. 218)

The conception that division "always makes smaller" is firmly ingrained in the minds of a large proportion of middle school aged children. When solving application problems, students develop an idea about the size of an answer relative to the numbers given in the problem. This idea then consistently influences the choice of the operation. This process does not serve well those students with poor estimation skills and misconceptions. (NCTM, 1993c, pp. 154–155)

Errors show that many students have learned rules for manipulating symbols without understanding what those symbols mean or why the rules work. Many students are unable to reason appropriately about symbols for rational numbers and do not have the strategic competence that would allow them to catch their mistakes. (NRC, 2001, p. 234)

There are important conceptual similarities between whole numbers and rational numbers when students learn to multiply and divide. The similarities are not apparent in the algorithms for manipulating the symbols. Therefore, if students are to connect what they are learning about rational numbers with what they already understand about whole numbers, they will need to do so through other kinds of activities. (NRC, 2001, p. 239)

Students can develop a deep understanding of rational numbers through experiences with a variety of models, such as number lines, 10×10 grids, area models, and other objects. These models offer students concrete representations of abstract ideas. (NCTM, 2000, p. 216)

Teaching Implications

To support a deeper understanding for students in middle school in regard to properties of multiplication and division as they relate to fractions and decimals, the following are ideas and questions to consider in conjunction with the research.

Focus Through Instruction

- Provide manipulatives and pictures to encourage modeling of the problem
- Provide a context for students to work with
- Focus on the meaning of the operation instead of just applying procedures to the numbers used in the problem
- Limit the size of the denominator used in problems initially

- Stress the reasonableness of the results once students have worked out the problem
- Help students deepen their understanding of rational numbers by presenting problems that call for flexible thinking

Questions to Consider . . . *when working with students as they grapple with these ideas*

- Do students continue to use what they know about the commutative and associative properties of addition and multiplication?
- Do students consider the reasonableness of their computation within a contextual presentation?
- Are students using flexible thinking as they consider that multiplication does not always make bigger?

Teacher Sound Bite

"I have always wondered why so many students have difficulty checking the results of their calculations with fractions and decimals. This probe has helped me realize that estimating requires conceptual understanding of the result of multiplying and dividing with decimals and that thinking "multiplication always makes bigger" can really get in the way of checking the reasonableness of an answer. I now spend more instructional time exploring the results of multiplying by a variety of numbers and having students look for patterns."

Additional References for Research and Teaching Implications

AAAS (1993), *Benchmarks for Science Literacy*, pp. 358–359.

NCTM (1993c), *Research Ideas for the Classroom: Middle Grades Mathematics*, pp. 150–155.

NCTM (2000), *Principles and Standards for School Mathematics*, pp. 216–218.

NRC (2001), *Adding It Up: Helping Children Learn Mathematics*, pp. 234–239.

Which Is Bigger?
Curriculum Topic Study
Related CTS Guide: Multiplication and Division

STUDENT RESPONSES TO "WHICH IS BIGGER?"

Sample Responses: ABBA

Student 1: All I did was mental multiplying and dividing.

Student 2: Multiplying is larger than dividing when you start with the same numbers.

Student 3: Multiplying means more, so I circled that.

(Continued)

(Continued)

> *Student 4:* I said that the problem with the star was larger because the star means multiply. And multiplication is always larger than division.
>
> *Student 5:* × is more, ÷ is less.
>
> *Student 6:* I knew that when you multiply the number increases. When you divide the number decreases.
>
> *Student 7:* Well, I know that ÷ is dividing and that * is multiplying.

Sample Response: AABA

> *Student 8:* I think because when you multiply it usually comes out to be larger than dividing. However, in the second problem, you're multiplying by a decimal so when multiplying it usually comes out 0.000 something. In number 4, I think they are equal because they're both fractions.

VARIATION: MULTIPLICATION MA[...]

"When you multiply, the answer is always bigger than any of the numbers in the problem."

"I think sometimes [...] answer is bigger, b[...] sometimes it isn't.[...]"

Erin   Tom

Which friend do you agree with?_____

Explain why you agree with one friend and disagree with the other. Provide evidence and/or examples that support your explanation.

_____

_____

_____

_____

_____

_____

_____

_____

_____

_____

VARIATION: WHICH IS BIGGER ? II

Use mental math and estimation to determine which problem results in the greatest answer.

  A. $100 + (-34.2)$

  B. $100 - (24.6)$

  C. 100×0.52

  D. $100 \div 0.24$

  Please explain your reasoning:

  _____

  _____

  _____

  _____

  _____

  _____

  _____

  _____

  _____

  _____

  _____

ARE YOU POSITIVE?

Probe
9

Using mental math, indicate which problems result in a *positive* answer.

A. $-(-53 + 92)$ ☐

B. $-34 - 27$ ☐

C. $93 - (-56)$ ☐

D. $(-24)(35)$ ☐

E. $(-34)(-54)$ ☐

F. $-34 + -56$ ☐

G. $\dfrac{-5}{-2}$ ☐

H. $\dfrac{-5-10}{-(-2)}$ ☐

   Describe the process that you used to decide whether the problem resulted in a positive answer,

TEACHERS' NOTES: ARE YOU POSITIVE?

Grade Level for "Are You Positive?" Probe

Grades K–2	3–5	6–8	9–12

*Q*uestioning for Student Understanding

Do students have an understanding of the meaning and effect of operations with negative numbers?

*U*ncovering Understandings

Are You Positive? Content Standard: Number and Operations
Variation: Are You Positive? Part II (excluding the rational expressions) and Are You Positive Part III (using decimal instead of integer examples).

*E*xamining Student Work

The distracters may reveal *common errors* regarding operations with negative numbers such as *overgeneralization* of *procedural* shortcuts or lack of *conceptual* understanding of meaning and effects of arithmetic operations with integers.

- *The correct response is C, E, and G.* Expression C is subtracting a negative integer, E is multiplying two negative integers, and G is dividing two negative integers. The typical trend in thinking about how to decide whether the expressions resulted in a positive answer is to use certain learned rules. (See Students 1 and 2 in *Student Responses* section.) These rules are sometimes called "shortcuts" and are often remembered or applied inaccurately as the responses to the distracters show.
- *Distracter A.* Students who choose A typically distribute the negative to the first integer inside the parenthesis but not to the second. (See Students 3 and 4 in *Student Responses* section.)
- *Distracter B.* Students who choose B most likely use the multiplication rule—two negatives multiplied together make a positive—but remember it as "two negatives make a positive." (See Student 6 in *Student Responses* section.) Others actually see this as a multiplication problem and use the rules for multiplication. (See Student 5 in *Student Responses* section.) Some students consider the negatives as canceling each other out. (See Student 3 in *Student Responses* section.)
- *Distracter D.* Many students who choose D see it as a problem involving not multiplication but addition. (See Student 7 in *Student Responses* section.) Others incorrectly think a negative times a positive is a positive. (See Student 8 in *Student Responses* section.)

- *Distracter F.* This distracter is similar to Distracter B. Students misuse a common shortcut about multiplying two negatives together to make a positive and overgeneralize this to "any two negatives make a positive." (See Students 6 and 9 in *Student Responses* section.) Some students count the negative signs and believe an even amount results in a positive answer. (See Student 10 in *Student Responses* section.)
- *Distracter H.* Students look at negatives being divided by negatives and think this results in a positive answer. (See Student 11 in *Student Responses* section.) Other students feel the negatives automatically "cancel each other out." (See Student 3 in *Student Responses* section.)

Seeking Links to Cognitive Research

Developing fluency requires a balance and connection between conceptual understanding and computational proficiency. Computational methods that are overpracticed without understanding are often forgotten or remembered incorrectly (Hiebert, 1999; Kamii, Lewis, and Livingston 1993; Hiebert and Lindquist 1990). (NCTM, 2000, p. 35)

Students misapply rules they have learned as isolated, mathematical procedures. The learning of facts and algorithms need[s] to be [a] building stone of the active mathematical knowledge of students. (NCTM, 2003, p.114)

Teaching Implications

To support a deeper understanding for students in middle school in regard to operations with negative numbers, the following are ideas and questions to consider in conjunction with the research.

Focus Through Instruction

- Students generally perform better on problems posed in the context of a story (debts and assets, scores and forfeits) or through movements on a number line than on the same problems presented solely as formal equations and expressions
- Students should spend ample time exploring appropriate models of integers and operations on integers to develop the rules and link them to the symbols
- The focus of classrooms should be to understand operations with negative numbers conceptually and to use a wide range of effective methods, not just isolated mathematical procedures
- Often when students learn the procedural rules for negative numbers as shortcuts for computation, many different kinds of errors arise, most of which are partially correct methods

Questions to Consider . . . *when working with students as they grapple with the idea of operations with negative numbers*

- Do students make sense of an answer within the context of the problem?
- Are students able to demonstrate operations that result in the same net value (i.e., subtracting a negative number and adding a positive number are different operations that result in the same answer)?
- Do students understand why the result of multiplying or dividing two negative numbers is a positive number?
- Do student overgeneralize the rules of operating with signed numbers?

Teacher Sound Bite

"Many students incorrectly transferred the shortcut of multiplying and dividing by negative numbers to addition and subtraction of negative numbers, even though we thoroughly discussed this in class. They seemed to understand addition and subtraction of negative numbers until they learned the "rule" for multiplication and division. I find that giving this probe and allowing students to discuss each of the problems results in a great class discussion. I find I do not need to reteach as the students work through the issue together."

Additional References for Research and Teaching Implications

Are You Positive?
Curriculum Topic Study
Related CTS Guide: Properties of Operations

AAAS (1993), *Benchmarks for Science Literacy*, pp. 210, 213, 288–289.

NCTM (1993c), *Research Ideas for the Classroom: Middle Grades Mathematics*, pp. 112–114.

NCTM (1999), *Algebraic Thinking*, pp. 18–19, 68.

NCTM (2000), *Principles and Standards for School Mathematics*, pp. 32–33, 35, 148, 152–156, 214, 220–221.

NCTM (2003), *Research Companion to Principles and Standards for School Mathematics*, pp. 71–72, 87–89, 114, 120–121.

NRC (2001), *Adding It Up: Helping Children Learn Mathematics* pp. 245–246.

STUDENT RESPONSES TO "ARE YOU POSITIVE?"

Sample Responses: CFH

Student 1: The way I knew whether it was positive or negative was because when you multiply two negatives you get a positive. When you multiply a positive and a negative, you get a negative. A positive minus a positive can go either way . . . and so on.

Student 2: A negative number multiplied or divided by another negative number is a positive. When adding a positive and a negative, you take the sign of the greatest absolute value.

Sample Responses: Other Combinations

Student 3: The negatives cancel each other out resulting in a positive.

Student 4: A negative on the outside of the parenthesis with a negative on the inside makes a positive.

Student 5: I used the rules of negatives . . . (−)(−) = +.

Student 6: The process I used was a negative plus a negative equals a positive and a negative subtracting a positive is a positive.

Student 7: If you have a negative number, you have to have a positive number that is bigger than the negative number to equal a positive number.

Student 8: negative × positive = positive.

Student 9: If there are two negatives, the answer will be positive. If there are two positives, then the answer will be positive, but if there is a negative and a positive, it will be negative.

Student 10: I looked to see how many negatives there were and if there was an even amount of them. If there's an even amount, it's positive. If there's an odd amount, it's negative.

Student 11: Negatives divided by negatives make positives.

VARIATION: ARE YOU POSITIVE? II

Using *mental math,* indicate which problems result in a *positive* answer.

A. $-(-24 + 78)$ ☐

B. $-24 - 17$ ☐

C. $92 - -51$ ☐

D. -34×62 ☐

E. -18×-26 ☐

F. $-35 + -56$ ☐

Describe the process that you used to decide whether the problem resulted in a positive answer,

VARIATION: ARE YOU POSITIVE? III

Probe
9b

Using *mental math,* decide which problems will result in a *positive* answer.

A. $-(-24.6 + 78.9)$ ☐

B. $-24.8 - 17.4$ ☐

C. $92.3 - (-51.6)$ ☐

D. -34.4×62.5 ☐

E. -18.4×-26.4 ☐

F. $-35.4 + -56.4$ ☐

Describe the process that you used to decide whether the problem resulted in a positive answer.

WHAT PERCENT IS THAT?

Probe 10

The following students used mental math to estimate 5.3% of 41.9.

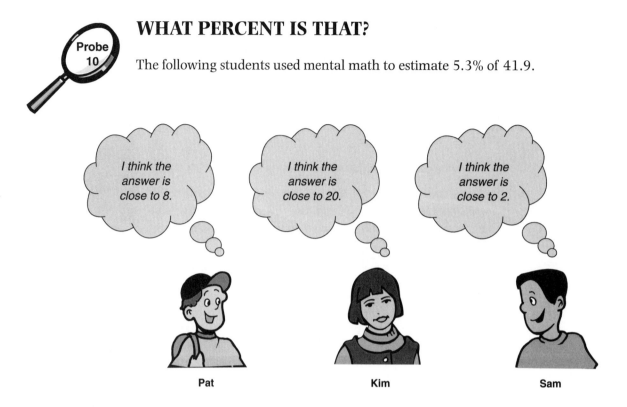

I think the answer is close to 8.

I think the answer is close to 20.

I think the answer is close to 2.

Pat

Kim

Sam

Who has the best estimate? Justify your answer by solving the problem correctly.

TEACHERS' NOTES: WHAT PERCENT IS THAT?

Grade Level for "What Percent Is That?" Probe

Grades K–2	3–5	6–8	9–12

*Q*uestioning for Student Understanding

Are students able to accurately estimate a percent of a number?

*U*ncovering Understandings

What Percent Is That? Content Standard: Number and Operations

*E*xamining Student Work

The distracters may reveal *common errors* when finding a percent of a number such as using the incorrect operation or not converting to a decimal or fraction before multiplying. In many cases, these *common errors* stem from a lack of *conceptual* understanding of percent.

- *The correct answer is Sam, who chose 2.* There are a variety of trends in correct thinking related to this probe, some of which are taking 1/20 of 40, multiplying 40 by .05, taking half of 10%, and using reasoning to rule out 8 and 20. Some students might correctly choose 2 with incorrect or partially correct reasoning. (See Students 1 and 2 in *Student Responses* section.)
- *Pat, who chose 8, is incorrect.* Many students choose this answer due to incorrectly dividing 40 by 8. (See Students 3 through 5 in *Student Responses* section.)
- *Kim, who chose 20, is incorrect.* Some students choose 20 for various reasons including misinterpreting 5% as taking .5% or taking half of the number. Others who chose this distracter understand that they should multiply 40 by .05 but are not able to carry out the multiplication correctly. In field testing, some students who correctly converted 5% to 1/20 went on to say the 1/20 of 40 is 20. (See Students 6 through 9 in *Student Responses* section.)

*S*eeking Links to Cognitive Research

Students may view percents simply as an alternative way of writing decimals or fractions rather than as special representations of relationships between two quantities. Overemphasis on equality between fraction, decimal, and percent forms masks the many meanings and uses of percents. (Bay Area Mathematics Task Force, 1999, p. 92)

Research on students' understanding of and ability to perform operations on fractions has shown disappointingly poor results. For example, researchers report that "children are going through the motions of operations with fractions, but they have not been exposed to the kinds of experiences that could provide them with necessary understandings." (NCTM, 1993c, p. 130)

When multiplying with decimal fractions, it is typical for student errors to be evenly split between the process of multiplication and the placement of the decimal. (NCTM, 1993c, p. 150)

In order to name a fractional part, the student must focus on the number of equal parts into which the whole has been partitioned and the number of those parts that are being considered. It is important to help students attach meaning to fraction symbols by encouraging them to connect their knowledge of an arrangement of manipulatives to symbols. (NCTM, 1993c, p. 125)

In grades 3–5, students should learn to generate equivalent forms of fractions, decimals, and percents in simple cases. In grades 6-8, students should build on and extend this experience to become facile in using fractions, decimals and percents meaningfully. (NCTM, 2000, p. 215)

Through discussions of problems in context, students can develop useful methods to compute with fractions, decimals, and percents in ways that make sense. Student's understanding of computation can be enhanced by developing their own methods and sharing them with one another, explaining why their methods work and are reasonable to use, and then comparing them to traditional algorithms. (NCTM, 2000, p. 220)

*T*eaching Implications

To support a deeper understanding for students in middle school in regard to percents, the following are ideas and questions to consider in conjunction with the research.

Focus Through Instruction

- Develop the concept that two quantities need to be known before establishing a percent
- Help students understand that percents represent general constant relationships
- Expose students to varied problems that relate two like quantities by percents
- Give students initial instruction in the relational language of percents before teaching calculation procedures
- Tie common percents to known benchmark fractions using a part-whole model, in addition to exploring the underlying ratios for percents
- Provide the idea that one purpose of percents, like ratios, is to make comparisons

Questions to Consider . . . *when working with students as they grapple with the idea of percents*

- Do students demonstrate an understanding of a percent in comparison to 100?
- When reading word problems, do students identify the parts of a percent relationship?
- Do students show an understanding of the relationship between ratios and percents?
- Do students connect the use of a percent with its role as a constant factor that can relate two quantities?

Teacher Sound Bite

"Before introducing the unit on computing with percents, I now first probe for student understanding of the meaning of percent. Without understanding the relationship between percents, decimals, and fractions, the taught procedures of setting up a proportion or converting to a decimal and multiplying, just don't make sense to students. Without a true understanding, there is no ability to check answers for reasonableness of the results."

Additional References for Research and Teaching Implications

Bay Area Mathematics Task Force (1999), *A Mathematics Source Book for Elementary and Middle School Teachers*, p. 92.

Griffin & Madgwick (2005), *Multiplication Makes Bigger and Other Mathematical Myths*, p. 8.

NCTM (1993c), *Research Ideas for the Classroom: Middle Grades Mathematics*, pp. 125–130, 150).

NCTM (2000), *Principles and Standards for School Mathematics*, pp. 215, 220.

What Percent Is That?
Curriculum Topic Study
Related CTS Guide: Percent

STUDENT RESPONSES TO "WHAT PERCENT IS THAT?"

Sample Responses: Sam

Student 1: Sam has the right answer.

Student 2: It is 2 because you take 100 and divide it by 5, which is 20. Then divide 20 by 40, and it equals 2.

Sample Responses: Pat

Student 3: Pat because 5 times 8 is 40.

Student 4: I agree with Pat because 20 is too high and 2 is too low.

Student 5: I think that Pat is right because 40 ÷ 5 = 8, and that is what Pat thought the answer was.

Sample Responses: Kim

Student 6: Kim because 5% is half. So if 5% is half then 40 = 20.

Student 7: I agree with Kim because 40 ÷ 5 is 20.

Student 8: I agree with Kim because if you take 40–5 it would be 35, and then you take 35 and subtract 15 to get 20.

Student 9: 40 × 5 is 200 but bring the decimal in for the percent and you get 20.

Algebra, Data Analysis, and Probability Assessment Probes

Key

███	Target for Instruction Based on National Standards and Cognitive Research
▒▒▒	Prerequisite Concept/Field Testing Indicates Student Difficulty

Question	Probe	Grade Span Bars			
		K–2	3–5	6–8	9–12
Chapter 4: Algebra, Data, and Probability					
What does the equals sign mean?	It's All About Balance	███	▒▒▒		
Do students understand that the equals sign symbolizes equivalence?	Seesaw	███	███▒		
Do students accurately use symbolic representation to make sense of the relationship being described?	Students Versus Teachers			███	▒▒▒
In thinking about rate of change graphically, do students understand how scale affects the presentation of a graph?	Rate of Change (Slope)			███	███▒
Are students able to identify linear relationships when represented symbolically?	Are They Linear?			███	███
Do students interpret graphs as literal pictures?	Distance From Home			███	▒▒▒
In thinking about probability, do students have a solid understanding of part-whole relationships?	Gumballs in a Jar		███		▒▒▒
Are students able to apply the concepts of compound probability?	The Spinners				███

IT'S ALL ABOUT BALANCE

Choose the correct answer for the following problem.

$$8 + 3 = \Box + 5$$

A. 16

B. 11

C. 6

Explain your thinking.

_____

_____

_____

_____

_____

_____

TEACHERS' NOTES: IT'S ALL ABOUT BALANCE

Grade Level for "It's All About Balance" Probe

Grades K–2	3–5	6–8	9–12

*Q*uestioning for Student Understanding

What does the equals sign mean?

*U*ncovering Understandings

It's All About Balance Content Standard: Algebra

*E*xamining Student Work

The distracters may reveal *common errors* regarding equivalence as it relates to solving equations with an unknown variable. The concept of equality is a crucial idea for developing algebraic reasoning in young children.

- *The correct answer is C.* The correct answer for the missing variable is 6. Students who choose C consider the value of 8 + 3 = 11 as it relates to 5 + n. (See Students 5, 6, and 7 in *Student Responses* section.)
- *Students who answer A.* Students who indicate choice A most likely add the 8 + 3 = 11 and then add 5 to get 16. Students see the equals sign as representing the end of an equation. (See Students 1 and 2 in *Student Responses* section.)
- *Students who answer B.* Students who indicate choice B consider the equals sign as coming at the end of an equation, allowing only one number to come after. (See Students 3 and 4 in *Student Responses* section.)

*S*eeking Links to Cognitive Research

Children in the elementary grades generally think that the equals sign means that they should carry out the calculation that precedes it and that the number after the equals sign is the answer to the calculation. Elementary school children generally do not see the equals sign as a symbol that expresses the relationship "is the same as." (NCTM, 2002, p. 203) Children must understand that equality is a relationship that expresses the idea that two mathematical expressions hold the same value. It is important for children to understand this idea for two reasons. First, children need this understanding to think about relationships expressed by number sentences. A second reason that understanding equality as a relationship is important is that a lack of such understanding is one of the major stumbling blocks for students when they move from arithmetic to algebra. (NCTM, 2002, p. 206)

The notion of equality also should be developed throughout the curriculum. As a consequence of the instruction they have received, young students typically perceive the equals sign operationally, that is, as a signal to "do something." They should come to view the equals sign as a symbol of equivalence and balance. (NCTM, 2000, p. 39)

In grades K–2, equality is an important algebraic concept that students must encounter and begin to understand. A common explanation for the equals sign given by students is that "the answer is coming" but they need to recognize that the equals sign indicates a relationship—that the quantities on each side are equivalent. (NCTM, 2000, p. 94)

In grades 3–5, the idea and usefulness of a variable (represented by a box, letter, or symbol) should also be emerging and developing more fully. As students explore patterns and note relationships, they should be encouraged to represent their thinking. (NCTM, 2000, p. 161)

*T*eaching Implications

To support a deeper understanding for students in elementary school in regard to equality, the following are ideas and questions to consider in conjunction with the research.

Focus Through Instruction

- Make direct comparisons between quantities by asking students about the relationship
- Offer varied representations denoting equivalence using the equals sign
- Use explicit language during instruction to refer to the equals sign as a relationship between two sides on an equation
- Use visual models that support the idea of equivalence (e.g., balance/seesaw)
- Embed symbolic representation and manipulation in instructional experiences to support sense making for students

- Provide opportunities for students to make connections from symbolic notation to the representation of an equation
- Use a balance and cubes to demonstrate equalities

Questions to Consider . . . when working with students as they grapple with the idea of equivalence

- Are students thinking about the equals sign as "the answer is coming"?
- Can students articulate the relationship between both sides of the equals sign in an equation?
- Are students representing the idea of equivalence through the development of their addition and subtraction strategies?

Teacher Sound Bite

"I never realized that although I talk about the equals sign in the context of balance, my students are not necessarily seeing the sign as a separator between two quantities and then considering the relationship between the two quantities."

Additional References for Research and Teaching Implications

Wearne & Hiebert (2001), *Putting Research Into Practice in the Elementary Grades*, pp. 203–206.

NCTM (1993a), *Research Ideas for the Classroom: Early Childhood Mathematics*, pp. 11–15.

NCTM (2000), *Principles and Standards for School Mathematics*, pp. 39, 94, 161.

NRC (2001), *Adding It Up: Helping Children Learn Mathematics*, pp. 261–263.

It's All About Balance
Curriculum Topic Study
Related CTS Guide: Equivalence

STUDENT RESPONSES TO "IT'S ALL ABOUT BALANCE"

Sample Responses: A

Student 1: I knew that 8 + 3 = 11, so I added 5 more to 11 and got 16.

Student 2: I added 8 + 3 + 5 = 16. I added it up by ones, and it equaled 16.

Sample Responses: B

Student 3: I found out this answer by adding 8 + 3 and got 11.

Student 4: I know this because 8 + 3 = 11 and the 5 is nothing, you do not use it at all.

Sample Responses: C

Student 5: 8 + 3 = 11, right, so just do the same thing with the five. 6 + 5 = 11. I got it by subtracting 1 from the 7 and getting 6. I added 6 to the 5 and got 11 just like 8 + 3 equals 11.

Student 6: I know that 5 is 2 larger than 3 so I made the number 6 because it is 2 less than 8.

Student 7: I added 8 and 3 together and got 11, then I take 5 away from that number. Then take what was left and added 5 to that number. 6 + 5 = 11.

SEESAW

Decide which of these statements are *True* and circle your choice(s).

A. $7 + 5 = 15$

B. $8 = 5 + 13$

C. $9 = 5 + 4$

D. $10 = 10$

E. $5 + 8 = 8 + 5$

F. $6 + 4 = 10$

For each one, how can you prove you are correct?

A.

B.

C.

D.

E.

F.

TEACHERS' NOTES: SEESAW

Grade Level for "Seesaw" Probe

Grades K–2	3–5	6–8	9–12

*Q*uestioning for Student Understanding

Do students understand that the equals sign symbolizes equivalence?

*U*ncovering Understandings

Seesaw Content Standard: Algebra

*E*xamining Student Work

The distracters may reveal *common errors* regarding equivalence, such as interpreting the equals sign to mean that a series of actions will be followed by a result or that the equals sign signals the result is coming.

- *The answers C, D, E, and F are true statements.* Examples C, D, E, and F all represent the idea of equality without being written in a standard equation format. Students who identified these as correct demonstrate *conceptual understanding* of the idea of equivalence (e.g., balance). (See Students 5 and 6 in *Student Responses* section.)
- *Students who answered F.* Students who choose F as the only true statement most likely understand the equals sign to represent the answer to a problem and are not focused on the idea of equivalence. (See Students 1 and 2 in *Student Responses* section.)
- *Students who answered C, D, and F.* Students who choose C, D, and F most likely consider the equals sign in each example but fail to recognize that Choice E is true as well because it has an equivalent expression on each side of the equals sign. (See Students 3 and 4 in *Student Responses* section.)

*S*eeking Links to Cognitive Research

Two central themes of algebraic thinking are appropriate for young students. The first involves making generalizations and using symbols to represent mathematical ideas, and the second is representing and solving problems. (NCTM, 2000, p. 93)

In the case of the equals sign the child should be led to recognize that several interpretations are valuable, especially the view of = as equivalence. The teacher's goal is to have the child learn the formal mathematical idea that the two sides of the equation are equivalent in number—for example, that the quantity 4 + 3 is the "same as" 7. Given that notion, you can then legitimately say that 7 = 4 + 3. (NCTM, 1993a, p. 13)

Children may have an appropriate understanding of equality relations involving collections of objects but have difficulty relating this understanding to symbolic representations involving the equal sign. (NCTM, 2002, pp. 202–203)

In grades K–2, equality is an important algebraic concept that students must encounter and begin to understand. A common explanation of the equals sign given by students is that "the answer is coming," but they need to recognize that the equals sign indicates a relationship— that the quantities on each side are equivalent, for example, 10 = 4 + 6 or 4 + 6 = 5 + 5 (NCTM, 2000, p. 94)

In grades 3–5, students who understand the structure of numbers and the relationship among numbers can work with them flexibly (Fuson, 1992). They recognize and can generate equivalent representations for the same number. (NCTM, 2000, p. 149)

As students become more experienced in investigating, articulating, and justifying generalizations, they can begin to use variable notation and equations to represent their thinking. Teachers will need to model how to represent thinking in the form of equations. In this way, they can help students connect the ways they are describing their findings to mathematical notation. (NCTM, 2000, pp. 161–162)

*T*eaching Implications

To support a deeper understanding for students in elementary school in regard to equality, the following are ideas and questions to consider in conjunction with the research.

Focus Through Instruction

- Make direct comparisons between quantities by asking students about the relationship
- Use varied representations denoting equivalence
- Use explicit language during instruction to refer to the equals sign as a relationship between two sides on an equation

- Use visual models that support the idea of equivalence (e.g., balance/ seesaw)
- Embed symbolic representation and manipulation in instructional experiences to support sense making for students
- Provide opportunities for students to make connections from symbolic notation to the representation of an equation
- Use a balance and cubes to demonstrate equalities

Questions to Consider . . . *when working with students as they grapple with the idea of equivalence*

- Are students thinking about the equals sign as "the answer is coming"?
- Can students articulate a relationship between both sides of the equals sign in an equation?
- Are students representing the idea of equivalence through the development of their addition and subtraction strategies?

Teacher Sound Bite

"It was eye-opening to present my students with this probe. I really felt like they would be very successful with choosing the correct answers. When we discussed the examples as a group, the students were very sure that both B and D were not equal because `that is not how we say a problem.' Now I think about representing equations in a variety of ways so students are not left believing that balance is related to how the equation is written versus the quantities on both sides."

Additional References for Research and Teaching Implications

Seesaw
Curriculum Topic Study
Related CTS Guide: Equality

NCTM (1993a), *Research Ideas for the Classroom: Early Childhood Mathematics*, pp. 11–15.

NCTM (2000), *Principles and Standards for School Mathematics*, pp. 93–94, 149, 161–162.

Wearne & Hiebert (2001), *Putting Research Into Practice in the Elementary Grades*, pp. 202–220.

STUDENT RESPONSES TO "SEESAW"

Sample Responses: F

Student 1: I know 6 + 4 = 10 because 6 + 2 = 8 and 8 + 2 = 10.

Student 2: I can prove I am correct because all the ones have 10 = 10 and that's not right. 10 + 0 = 10 is right but that's not a choice. So I think 6 + 4 = 10 is the right one because the other ones have mistakes.

Sample Responses: CDF

Student 3: I know that 5 + 4 = 9 because I counted on my fingers. I know that 10 = 10, too. I know that 6 + 4 = 10 because I counted on my fingers.

Student 4: The way I know is because if you put 4 + 5 together you get 9. If you put 6 + 4 together you get 10. 10 = 10.

Sample Responses: CDEF

Student 5: I know that 5 + 4 = 9 so C is right. I know that 10 equals itself. I know that 5 + 8 equals the same as 8 + 5—they are just switched around. I know that 6 + 4 = 10 because it's a tens fact.

Student 6: I know that 10 = 10 because they are both the same number. I know that 5 + 8 = 8 + 5 because it's the same thing, just backwards. I added 5 + 4 and got 9 and 6 + 4 and got 10.

STUDENTS VERSUS TEACHERS

Which equation represents the following statement?

"There are 6 times as many students as teachers in the room today."

Let s = the number of students

Let t = the number of teachers

A. $6s = t$

B. $6t = s$

C. $st = 6$

Explain your choice:

_____

_____

_____

_____

_____

_____

_____

_____

_____

TEACHERS' NOTES: STUDENTS VERSUS TEACHERS

Grade Level for "Students Versus Teachers" Probe

Grades K–2	3–5	6–8	9–12

Questioning for Student Understanding

Do students accurately use symbolic representation to make sense of the relationship being described?

Uncovering Understandings

Students Versus Teachers Content Standard: Algebra
Variation: Students Versus Teachers II (using multiple selections format) and Students Versus Teachers III (using examples and nonexamples format)

Examining Student Work

The distracters may reveal a lack of *conceptual* understanding of the use of variables and equations to represent relationships.

- *The correct response is B.* Students who correctly choose B are using variables to represent numbers (numbers of students and teachers). They translate the mathematical relationship into an equation, making sense of the words. (See Students 1 and 2 in *Student Responses* section.)
- *Distracter A.* Students who choose this option typically use a direct translation of the words into an algebraic equation without understanding the relationship described. It is most likely that students are using variables to represent words. The formula $6s = t$ is the result of changing "six times as many students" into "six times the number of students" (NCTM, 1993b, p. 95). (See Students 3, 4, and 5 in *Student Responses* section.)
- *Distracter C.* Generally, this option is chosen only by students who do not know where to go in translating this into an algebraic equation and show no understanding of the relationship being described. (See Students 6 and 7 in *Student Responses* section.)

Seeking Links to Cognitive Research

The concept of a variable, pervasive as it is in mathematics, is difficult and often not understood. Letter names for variables may be taken to stand for single units (P to stand for professor rather than some number of professors). (AAAS, 1993, p. 219)

Research indicates a variety of student difficulties with the concept of variable (Kuchemann 1978; Kieran 1983; Wagner and Parker, 1993), so developing understanding of variable over the grades is important. In the elementary grades, students typically develop a notion of variable as a placeholder for a specific number, as in __ + 2 = 11. Later they should learn that the variable x in the equation 3x + 2 = 11 has a very different use from the variable x in the identity 0 * x = 0 and that both uses are quite different from the use of r in the formula $A = \pi r^2$. A thorough understanding of variable develops over a long time, and it needs to be grounded in extensive experience (Sfard, 1991). (NCTM, 2000, p. 39)

Students have difficulty understanding how symbols are used in algebra (Kieran, 1992). They are often unaware of the arbitrariness of the letters chosen to represent variables in equations (Wagner, 1981). Middle and high school students may regard the letters as shorthand for single objects, or as specific but unknown numbers, or as generalized numbers before they understand them as representations of variables (Kieran, 1992). (AAAS, 1993, p. 351)

*T*eaching Implications

To support a deeper understanding for students in middle school in regard to symbolic representation, the following are ideas and questions to consider in conjunction with the research.

Focus Through Instruction

- Provide extensive experience in interpreting relationships among quantities in a variety of problem contexts before working with variables and expressions
- Develop the concept of variables over the grades and ground it in extensive experience through real-world situations familiar and interesting to students before abstract definition
- Have students define variables and encourage students to look for the relationship between variables based on their definition
- Provide opportunities for students to use other forms of representation (tables, graphs) to make decisions about accurate algebraic representations
- Have students write descriptive statements for different relations to help address multiple word arrangements
- Use group discussions as a means for students to reach consensus about the meaning of words and relationships between variables

Questions to Consider . . . *when working with students as they grapple with the idea of symbolic representation*

- Are students able to describe the relationship in words?
- Do students define the variable in terms of "the number of _____"?
- Do students make sense of equations based on the given context?
- Are students able to describe the relationship within tables and graphs?

Teacher Sound Bite

"This has been one of the hardest concepts for my students. After I talked to other teachers, we have decided to take a deeper look at our K–12 curriculum to see how variables are taught so we have a better understanding of what our students are learning over many years. This probe helped us to tackle this issue as a district and not as individual teachers."

Additional References for Research and Teaching Implications

AAAS (1993), *Benchmarks for Science Literacy,* pp. 215, 218–221, 351.

NCTM (1993b), *Research Ideas for the Classroom: High School Mathematics,* pp. 95, 111, 122–123.

NCTM (1999), *Algebraic Thinking,* pp. 7–13, 52–70, 157–162, 321–327, 330.

NCTM (2000), *Principles and Standards for School Mathematics* (Algebra), pp. 37–39, 161–162, 225–227, 300.

NCTM (2001b), *Navigating Through Algebra in Grades 9–12,* pp. 13–21.

NCTM (2002), *Reflecting on NCTM's Principles and Standards in Elementary and Middle School Mathematics,* pp. 132–134.

NCTM (2003), *Research Companion to Principles and Standards for School Mathematics,* pp. 123–133.

NCTM (2006a), *Teachers Engaged in Research,* pp. 104–109.

NRC (2001), *Adding It Up: Helping Children Learn Mathematics,* pp. 263–270.

Students Versus Teachers
Curriculum Topic Study
Related CTS Guide: Variables

STUDENT RESPONSES TO "STUDENTS VERSUS TEACHERS"

Sample Responses: B

Student 1: The answer is B. I checked it with a t-table, and it was the only one that worked correctly.

Student 2: The number of students is 6 times the number of teachers so it has to be $s = 6t$.

Sample Responses: A

Student 3: 6s means 6 times as many students and that is = to the amount of teachers.

Student 4: There are more students than teachers so the 6 needs to be with the *s.*

Student 5: I tried to convert the words into numbers.

Sample Responses: C

Student 6: I guessed.

Student 7: I know you need to use multiplication, and C has *s* and *t* being multiplied.

VARIATION: STUDENTS VERSUS TEACHERS II

1. Which equation accurately represents the following statement:

"There are 14 more students than teachers in the room today"

Let s = the number of students

Let t = the number of teachers

A. $t + 14 = s$

B. $s + 14 = t$

C. $s + t = 14$

Explain your choice:

_____

_____

_____

_____

_____

_____

2. Which equation accurately represents the following statement:

"There are 6 times as many students as teachers in the room today."

Let s = the number of students

Let t = the number of teachers

A. $6s = t$

B. $6t = s$

C. $st = 6$

Explain your choice:

_____

_____

_____

_____

_____

_____

VARIATION: STUDENTS VERSUS TEACHERS III

Probe 3b

Which equations accurately represent the following statement:

"There are 6 times as many students as teachers in the room today."

Let *s* represent the number of students

Let *t* represent the number of teachers

A. $6s = t$ ☐   B. $6t = s$ ☐

C. $s = 6t$ ☐   D. $t = 6s$ ☐

E. $\dfrac{6}{t} = s$ ☐   F. $\dfrac{s}{6} = t$ ☐

G. $st = 6$ ☐   H. $\dfrac{t}{6} = s$ ☐

I. $\dfrac{1}{6}s = t$ ☐   J. $\dfrac{1}{6}t = s$ ☐

Explain your process:

RATE OF CHANGE (SLOPE)

Circle the letter of each graph that shows a rate of change of 1.

A.

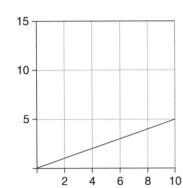

B.

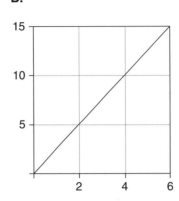

C.

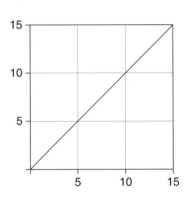

D.

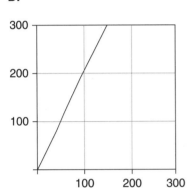

E.

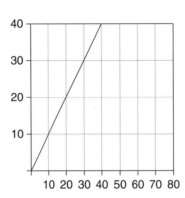

F.

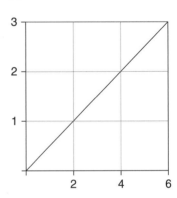

Explain what helped you make your decision.

_____

_____

_____

_____

_____

TEACHERS' NOTES:
RATE OF CHANGE (SLOPE)

Grade Level for "Rate of Change (Slope)" Probe

Grades K–2	3–5	6–8	9–12

*Q*uestioning for Student Understanding

In thinking about rate of change graphically, do students understand how scale affects the presentation of a graph?

*U*ncovering Understandings

Rate of Change (Slope) Content Standards: Algebra and Measurement
Variation: Rate of Change (Slope) Part II (using lines that do not all go through the origin)

*E*xamining Student Work

The distracters may reveal *common errors* regarding rate of change such as focusing on appearance of the graph, lack of *conceptual* understanding of rate of change and scale, or lack of *procedural* understanding of ways to determine a slope of one, such as "rise over run" and "up one over one."

- *The correct response is C and E.* Graphs C and E have a rate of change of one. Both graphs have the same x and y scales, but Graph E has a different viewing window. Some trends in thinking about how to find a rate of change are: rise/run, "up one over one," and slope formula. Another technique, based on whether the x and y coordinates are the same, might show only a partial understanding as each line goes through the origin. An additional probe (see Variations) that might be given to these students would show a variety of lines, all of which do not go through the origin. (See Students 1, 2, and 3 in *Student Responses* section.)
- *Distracter A.* Students who choose A observe that the line is only in the first row, and therefore, they misinterpret this to indicate a rate of change of one. Their trend in thinking is that the line goes up "one box" or one row and that this represents a rate of change of one. (See Students 4 and 5 in *Student Responses* section.)
- *Distracter B.* Students who choose B most likely fail to see the difference in the x and y scales. They use the "up one over one" rule to misinterpret a rate of change of one. (See Students 6, 7, and 8 in *Student Responses* section.) Many students interpret a 45° angle to represent a rate of change of one without consideration of the x and y scale. (See Students 9 and 10 in *Student Responses* section.)

- *Distracter D.* Students who choose D typically see the x and y scales both increasing by the same number (100) and believe this to represent a rate of change of one. Many students who use this reasoning also choose C and E. (See Student 11 in *Student Responses* section.)
- *Distracter F.* There are two trends in thinking for Choice F. Some students choose F for the same reason as Distracter B. Other students choose F because the y axis scale goes "up" by one, and they perceive this as a rate of change of one. (See Student 12 in *Student Responses* section.)

Seeking Links to Cognitive Research

When interpreting graphs, middle-school students do not understand the effect that a scale change would have on the appearance of the graph (Kerslake, 1981). (AAAS, 1993, p. 351)

The distinguishing quality of graphs that sets them apart from other standard mathematical representations is that they are a visual medium. Although the visual aspect—the visuality—of graphs makes them an extremely rich and powerful medium for generating meaning, it is also the source of many of the incorrect responses students have to graphs. (NCTM, 2003, p. 256)

Teaching Implications

To support a deeper understanding for students in middle school in regard to rate of change, the following are ideas and questions to consider in conjunction with the research.

Focus Through Instruction

- Provide opportunities for students to develop and explore change in the context of the science, mathematics, or technology being studied
- Develop an understanding that linear functions have a constant rate of change
- Provide experiences with graphs that are oriented in various positions and scales to aid students in forming generalizations that will not be bound to "standard" orientations and scales
- Give students experiences with graphing tools such as computers and graphing calculators, and allow them to explore graphical representations with them
- Allow students to explore many different slopes, y-intercepts, scales, and window settings, and have them engage in discussions on the effects that each has on the appearance and presentation of graphs

Questions to Consider . . . *when working with students as they grapple with the idea of rate of change*

- Do students understand the effect of scale on the representation of the data?
- Are students able to describe how the slope and y-intercept relates to a given context?
- Are students exposed to a variety of orientations, scales, slopes, and y-intercepts?

Teacher Sound Bite

"I was very surprised to see how many misconceptions my students have regarding slope. The results of this probe helped me plan my instruction to better fit my students' needs. I now include a variety of scales in examples as well as provide a context in which students can discuss situations where the rate is the same but the data points, scale, and intervals of the graph differ greatly."

Additional References for Research and Teaching Implications

AAAS (1993), *Benchmarks for Science Literacy*, pp. 216–220, 271–275, 351.

NCTM (1993b), *Research Ideas for the Classroom: High School Mathematics*, pp. 114–115.

NCTM (1993c), *Research Ideas for the Classroom: Middle Grades Mathematics*, p. 94.

NCTM (1999), *Algebraic Thinking*, pp. 22–30, 35.

NCTM (2000), *Principles and Standards for School Mathematics* (Algebra, Grades 6–8), p. 229, (Grades 9–12) p. 247; (Measurement, Grades 6–8) p. 305, (Grades 9–12) p. 321.

NCTM (2001a), *Navigating Through Algebra in Grades 6–8*, pp. 19–26.

NCTM (2003), *Research Companion to Principles and Standards for School Mathematics*, pp. 136–148, 252–260.

> **Rate of Change (Slope)**
>
> *Curriculum Topic Study*
>
> Related CTS Guide:
> Rate of Change

STUDENT RESPONSES TO "RATE OF CHANGE (SLOPE)"

Sample Responses: CE

Student 1: I looked at each one that went up one over one with the same scales on the x and y axes.

Student 2: Because 5/5 = 1 and 10/10 = 1.

Student 3: I used the slope formula, and C and E are the only ones that came out to 1.

Sample Responses: A

Student 4: I chose A because the line is only in the first row of boxes.

Student 5: I chose A because it moved one line up even though it started at 0 and went to 5.

Sample Responses: BCEF

Student 6: Because you go up one over one to find the slope, and if the lines meet the points, it's 1.

Student 7: I choose these graphs because they all met at a point that you could mark without drawing one.

Student 8: I circled these four because each line goes up by one square each.

Sample Responses: BCF

Student 9: I knew because slopes of 1 draw a line directly from the origin to the top righthand box and cut the corner in two. Since B, C, and F are all doing that, they have slopes of 1.

Student 10: What helped me make my decision was they are in a straight line from corner to corner.

Sample Response: CDE

Student 11: Both the x and y go up by the same number. This means they are both the same, and the line has a slope of one.

Sample Response: F

Student 12: When I looked at Graph F, I noticed that the y scale increased by one every line up.

VARIATION: RATE OF CHANGE (SLOPE) II

Probe
4a

Circle the letter of each graph that shows a rate of change of 1.

A.

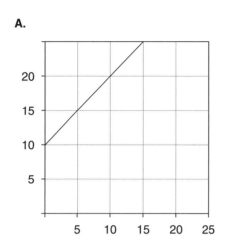

B.

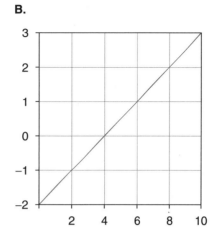

C.

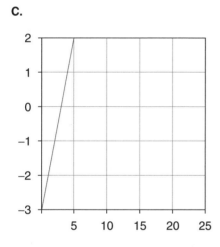

D.

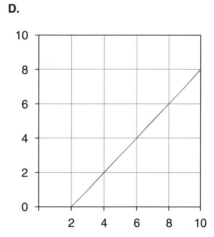

Explain your reasoning for each.

_____

_____

_____

_____

_____

_____

_____

ARE THEY LINEAR?

Circle the letters of each of the examples showing a linear equation.

A. $3x + 5y - 2 = 2y + 4$ B. $x = 9y - 12$

C. $(x+2)^2 - x^2 = y$ D. $y^2 = 7x + 15$

E. $y = x^3 - x + 3$ F. $4x^2 + x - 6 = 2(2x^2 - 3x + 7)$

For each example, explain or show how you know it does or does not show a linear equation.

A.

B.

C.

D.

E.

F.

TEACHERS' NOTES: ARE THEY LINEAR?

Grade Level for "Are They Linear?" Probe

Grades K–2	3–5	6–8	9–12

Questioning for Student Understanding

Are students able to identify linear relationships when represented symbolically?

Uncovering Understandings

Are They Linear? Content Standards: Algebra and Representation

Examining Student Work

The distracters may reveal *common errors* about how linear equations are symbolically represented and the *overgeneralization* of looking for first degree equations.

- *The correct responses are A, B, C, and F.* All of these equations are examples of linear equations. Several are written in forms other than the standard or slope-intercept forms of linear equations. (See Students 1 and 2 in *Student Responses* section.)
- *Distracter A.* Students who do not choose A typically see the variable y on both sides of the equation and do not see this as linear. (See Student 6 in *Student Responses* section.)
- *Distracter B.* Some students eliminate this example because y is not "alone" on one side, as in slope-intercept form. (See Students 3 and 4 in *Student Responses* section.)
- *Distracter C.* Typically, if students see an exponent other than one, they assume that it is not a linear equation. In this case, when everything is distributed and simplified, there are no x^2 terms. (See Student 5 in *Student Responses* section.) Others feel this equation is linear because there is a y alone on one side, which might not always be the correct reasoning. (See Students 3 and 4 in *Student Responses* section.)
- *Distracter D.* This distracter does not have an x term with a degree higher than one, but the y term is squared. Students see the y "alone" on one side of the equation and believe this is solved for y, and therefore linear. (See Students 3, 4, 6, and 7 in *Student Responses* section.)
- *Distracter E.* This case is similar to Distracter D. Students see that y is solved for and believe it to be in linear form. They fail to recognize the squared term as representing a quadratic equation. (See Students 3, 4, and 7 in *Student Responses* section.)

- *Distracter F.* This example is also one that, when simplified, no longer has an x^2 term. Students automatically see the squared term and decide it is not linear. (See Student 5 in *Student Responses* section.) Other students notice that there are like variables on opposite sides of the equation and think this cannot be linear. (See Student 6 in *Student Responses* section.) Some students notice that there are not two variables in the equation and decide it cannot be linear without both an x and a y. They fail to consider a vertical line. (See Students 6 and 7 in *Student Responses* section.)

Seeking Links to Cognitive Research

In general, if students engage extensively in symbolic manipulation before they develop a solid conceptual foundation for their work, they will be unable to do more than mechanical manipulations. The foundation for meaningful work with symbolic notation should be laid over a long time. (NCTM, 2000, p. 39)

[Middle grades students] should be able to distinguish linear relationships from nonlinear ones. [They] should learn to recognize and generate equivalent expressions, solve linear equations, and use simple formulas. (NCTM, 2000, p. 223)

The study of linear functions, with the associated patterns and relationships, is a major focus in the middle grades. By considering problems in a variety of contexts, students should become familiar with a range of representations for linear relationships, including tables, graphs, and equations. Students need to learn to use these representations flexibly and appropriately. (NCTM, 2000, p. 282)

Teaching Implications

To support a deeper understanding for students in middle school in regard to linear functions, the following are ideas and questions to consider in conjunction with the research.

Focus Through Instruction

- Give students early experiences with variables used in general relationships so that variables are not seen as representing only "unknown" or "missing" quantities
- Provide experiences with data from a relationship that is expressed verbally, in a table, on a graph, and as a symbolic rule (equation)
- Provide experiences with graphing technology to allow an alternative approach to linear functions
- Develop the concept of a variable by first looking at a variety of numerical replacements and gradually discussing variables as representing a range of values
- Give students in-depth experiences with real-life functional relationships between two quantities, and then express the relationships using variables

- Look for a constant rate of change in the dependent variable when examining data in a table

Questions to Consider . . . *when working with students as they grapple with the idea of linear functions*

- Do students demonstrate an understanding of the equal sign as equality between two sides of an equation?
- Can students write several possible equations for a situation?
- Are students generalizing arithmetic conventions with algebraic conventions?
- Do students define variables and use precise language in speaking about their algebraic thinking?

Teacher Sound Bite

"Many of my students' responses showed me they misunderstood what a first degree equation is. I need to have my students work with different representations for the same equation so that they see what happens when the equation is simplified."

Additional References for Research and Teaching Implications

AAAS (1993), *Benchmarks for Science Literacy*, pp. 215–216, 218–220.
NCTM (1993b), *Research Ideas for the Classroom: High School Mathematics*, pp. 126–128, 132–133.
NCTM (1999), *Algebraic Thinking*, pp. 17, 36, 84, 158–160, 215–219.
NCTM (2000), *Principles and Standards for School Mathematics*, pp. 37, 39, 67–71, 162, 207–208, 223, 282–285.
NCTM (2003), *Research Companion to Principles and Standards for School Mathematics*, pp. 123–124, 126–128.
NCTM (2006a), *Teachers Engaged in Research*, pp. 97–118.

Are They Linear?
Curriculum Topic Study
Related CTS Guide: Symbolic Representation

STUDENT RESPONSES TO "ARE THEY LINEAR?"

Sample Responses: ABCF

Student 1: I chose A, B, C, and F because all of them are first degree equations. Some don't look like it at first, but when you simplify them they are.

Student 2: When you solve the problems out (simplify), the final answer is to the degree of 1 for both variables.

Sample Responses: Other Combinations

Student 3: Because it is in the y = mx + b format.

Student 4: I decided by circling the ones that have to equal y.

Student 5: I chose A and B because the rest of the equations are more than first degree equations. They have exponents more than 1.

Student 6: I know that in linear equations you need two variables. Also, you can only have like variables on the same side.

Student 7: I decided which ones to circle because I thought that linear equations were ones that have both x and y in them.

DISTANCE FROM HOME

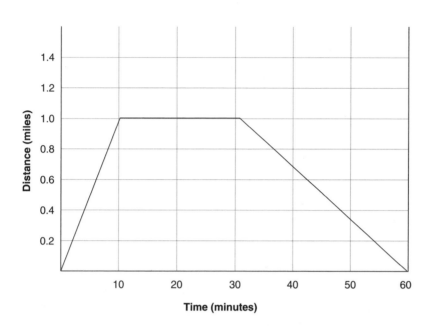

The graph shown above represents a person's round trip walk to a store starting from home. Choose the sentence that best describes the trip.

A. The person walked uphill, then on a flat surface, then downhill.

B. The person walked uphill to the store, stopped, then walked downhill to get home.

C. The person walked toward the store, stopped, then walked back home.

Explain what helped you make your decision.

_____

_____

_____

_____

_____

TEACHERS' NOTES: DISTANCE FROM HOME

Grade Level for "Distance From Home" Probe

Grades K–2	3–5	6–8	9–12
		███	░░░

Questioning for Student Understanding

Do students interpret graphs as literal pictures?

Uncovering Understandings

Distance From Home Content Standards: Algebra and Representation

Examining Student Work

The distracters may reveal *common errors* regarding distance-time graphs such as viewing the graph as a literal picture. This can sometimes be attributed to a lack of *conceptual* understanding of the relationship between distance and time and/or the meaning of rate of change.

- *The correct response is C.* The graph shows the distance a person is from home as he is walking toward the store, at the store, and walking back home. (See Students 1, 2, 3, and 4 in *Student Responses* section.)
- *Distracter A.* Students who choose A typically see the graph as a literal picture of a hill and see the graph depicting someone walking uphill, then on a flat surface, then downhill. They fail to see the relationship between time and distance and the meaning of rate of change (slope) in the graph. (See Students 5, 6, and 7 in *Student Responses* section.)
- *Distracter B.* Students who choose B are generally beginning to understand the relationship between time and distance (e.g., that between 10 and 30 minutes, the person stopped), although they still see the graph as a picture of a hill and the rate of change (slope) as the steepness of the hill. (See Students 8, 9, and 10 in *Student Responses* section.)

Seeking Links to Cognitive Research

Students of all ages often interpret graphs of situations as literal pictures rather than as symbolic representations of the situations (Leinhardt, Zaslavsky, & Stein, 1990; McDermott, Rosenquist, & van Zee, 1987). Many students interpret distance/time graphs as the paths of actual journeys (Kerslake, 1981). (AAAS, 1993, p. 351)

Among the most widely agreed upon conclusions of research on graphing in the last 25 years is that visuality is a key source of difficulties for students using graphs. "Iconic interpretation," that is, interpreting a graph as a literal picture, and other inappropriate responses to visual attributes of a graph are "the most frequently cited student errors with respect to interpreting and constructing graphs" (Leinhardt, Zaslavsky, & Stein, 1990, p. 39). (NCTM, 2003, p. 257)

*T*eaching Implications

To support a deeper understanding for students in middle school in regard to graphic representation, the following are ideas and questions to consider in conjunction with the research.

Focus Through Instruction

- Provide multiple opportunities for students to construct and critique graphs, which will help reveal what students understand or misunderstand about graphs and graphing
- Explore the relationship between a graph and a verbal statement before looking at a table or an algebraic representation
- Have students make up stories about different graphs and have discussions on the accuracy of the connections to real life situations
- Use motion detectors to learn about graphs of position versus time, linking students' kinesthetic, narrative, and visual capacities in their understanding of mathematics
- Allow students to collect and display their own data, which will enable them to rely on their own experiences when analyzing similar situations
- Discuss common errors and misconceptions with students; this strategy is more effective than to avoid exposing the errors
- Give students many opportunities to discuss their ideas and thinking strategies about graphs and functions so they can develop their interpretive skills

Questions to Consider . . . *when working with students as they grapple with the idea of graphic representation*

- Are students able to choose the correct graph when given a context?
- Do students consider the labels when analyzing a graph?
- Are students able to create a graph when given a situation or after collecting data?
- Are students viewing graphs as symbolic representations of a given situation rather than as a literal picture?

Teacher Sound Bite

"The instructional implications based on my students' responses are very important. I will definitely spend more time having students describe what they see happening in different graphs. I will have them tell me stories of what they see in graphs and have more group discussions of the meanings of graphs."

Additional References for Research and Teaching Implications

AAAS (1993), *Benchmarks for Science Literacy*, pp. 296–297, 351.

NCTM (1993b), *Research Ideas for the Classroom: High School Mathematics*, pp. 83–86, 92–94, 114–115.

NCTM (1993c), *Research Ideas for the Classroom: Middle Grades Mathematics*, pp. 91–93.

NCTM (1999), *Algebraic Thinking*, pp. 34–35, 215–219, 225–230, 275–279, 334–336.

NCTM (2000), *Principles and Standards for School Mathematics*, pp. 38, 41, 48–49, (Grades 3–5) pp. 167, 178, 206–209, (Grades 6–8) pp. 223–225, 229–230, 282, (Grades 9–12) pp. 305, 362–364.

NCTM (2001a), *Navigating Through Algebra in Grades 6–8*, pp. 19–35.

NCTM (2003), *Research Companion to Principles and Standards for School Mathematics*, pp. 250–260.

Shell Centre for Mathematics Education & Joint Matriculation Board (1985), *The Language of Functions and Graphs*, pp. 6, 203–230.

Van Dyke (2002), *A Visual Approach to Functions*.

Distance From Home
Curriculum Topic Study
Related CTS Guide: Graphic Representation

STUDENT RESPONSES TO "DISTANCE FROM HOME"

Sample Responses: C

Student 1: C is the only one that makes logical sense. How can you determine the terrain from the speed at which you walk?

Student 2: I made my decision by looking at the time and distance. For 10 minutes, this person walked 1 mile. Then for 20 minutes she stayed at 1 mile (that means that she didn't walk). When she walked back home, it took her 30 minutes to walk 1 mile.

Student 3: It doesn't say anywhere about hills. It says distance and time.

Student 4: When they were walking to the store, they didn't have to carry anything. Then they stayed at the store to shop. They walked home slower because they were carrying groceries.

Sample Responses: A

Student 5: Because it shows it going uphill, then on a flat surface, then downhill.

Student 6: It is what the grid looks like, but the distance and time have nothing to do with the terrain.

Student 7: The shape of the lines helped me make my decision. Also, we don't know if, when the person got to the top of the hill, they got to the store. We also don't know if they ever stopped. All we truly know is that they walked uphill, on a flat surface, and then downhill.

Sample Responses: B

Student 8: Because they went fast, then stopped, then went slower.

Student 9: Because the graph goes uphill, then stopped, then down.

Student 10: I chose this because the distance stays the same on the flat part because the person stopped at the store.

GUMBALLS IN A JAR

Two jars hold black and white gumballs.

Jar A: 3 black and 2 white

Jar B: 6 black and 4 white

Jar A   **Jar B**

Which statement best describes the chance of getting a *black* gumball?

A. There is a better chance of getting a black gumball from Jar A.

B. There is a better chance of getting a black gumball from Jar B.

C. The chance of getting a black gumball is the same
    for both Jar A and Jar B.

Explain your reason for the statement you selected.

_____

_____

_____

_____

_____

_____

_____

_____

TEACHERS' NOTES: GUMBALLS IN A JAR

Grade Level for "Gumballs in a Jar" Probe

Grades K–2	3–5	6–8	9–12

Questioning for Student Understanding

In thinking about probability, do students have a solid understanding of part-whole relationships?

Uncovering Understandings

Gumballs in a Jar Content Standard: Data Analysis and Probability
Variations: Gumballs in a Jar II (one jar for Grades 3 through 5) and Gumballs in a Jar III (nondoubling variation for Grades 7 through 12)

Examining Student Work

The distracters may reveal *common errors* regarding probability such as focusing on absolute size or a lack of *conceptual* understanding of probability as a prediction of what is likely to happen.

- *The correct answer is C.* There is the same chance you will pick a black gumball out of each jar. Jar A has a probability of 3/5 and Jar B has a probability of 6/10 = 3/5. There are a variety of trends in correct thinking related to this probe, some of which are: doubling, ratios, and percents. (See Students 1 and 2 in *Student Responses* section.) Some students might correctly choose C with incorrect reasoning, such as "You can't know for sure since anything can happen," which indicates lack of *conceptual* understanding of probability. Other students may demonstrate partial understanding with responses such as "Each jar has more black than white." (See Students 3 and 4 in *Student Responses* section.)
- *Distracter A.* Some students reason that there are fewer white gumballs in Jar A compared to Jar B and therefore a better chance of picking a black gumball from Jar A. (See Student 5 in *Student Responses* section.) These students focus on absolute size instead of relative size in comparing the likelihood of events. Students sometimes choose Distracter A due to an error in counting or calculation. (See Student 6 in *Student Responses* section.)
- *Distracter B.* Students observe Jar B as having more black gumballs compared to Jar A and conclude that there is a better chance of picking a

black gumball. These students focus on absolute size instead of relative size in comparing the likelihood of events. (See Students 7 and 8 in *Student Responses* section.)

Seeking Links to Cognitive Research

[Jones, Langrall, Thorton, and Mogill] theorized that children exhibit four levels of thinking about probability situations: subjective, transitional, informal quantitative, and numerical. (NCTM, 2003, p. 217)

[The Outcome Approach] Students might not possess a process model for chance experiments, because they do not envision the results of a single trial of an experiment as just one of many possible outcomes that will vary across a sample space if the experiment is repeated. (NCTM, 2003, p. 218)

Teaching Implications

To support a deeper understanding for students in middle school in regard to probability, the following are ideas and questions to consider in conjunction with the research.

Focus Through Instruction

- Students should learn about probability as a measurement of the likelihood of events
- Students should explore probability through experiments that have only a few outcomes
- Computer simulations provide a quick method of collecting large samples in providing experimental data that is close to the theoretical probability
- To correct misconceptions, it is helpful for students to make predictions and then compare the predictions with actual outcomes
- Students should encounter the idea that although they can't determine an individual outcome, they can predict the frequency of various outcomes
- A solid understanding of ratio and proportion is critical for understanding relative frequency
- In Grades 3 through 5, students should use common fractions to represent the probability of a certain event

Questions to Consider . . . *when working with students as they grapple with the idea of probability*

- Do the students focus on relative size when calculating probabilities?
- Do students view probability as a prediction of what is likely to happen?
- Over time, are students able to make predictions based on what is likely to happen?

Teacher Sound Bite

"As a fourth-grade teacher, I now follow up with a numeric answer when dealing with probability of a single event. I too often leave it as more space, or equal amount, etc. Although using the words is a good start in beginning stages of instruction, the ratio is important as both evidence and representation and would allow students to transfer from single events to comparing two or more events."

Additional References for Research and Teaching Implications

NCTM (1993b), *Research Ideas for the Classroom: High School Mathematics*, pp. 177–194.

NCTM (1993c), *Research Ideas for the Classroom: Middle Grades Mathematics*, pp. 6, 83–87.

NCTM (2000), *Principles and Standards for School Mathematics*, pp. 181, 254.

NCTM (2003), *Research Companion to Principles and Standards for School Mathematics*, p. 217.

Stavy & Tirosh (2000), *How Students (Mis-)Understand Science and Mathematics*, pp. 1–2, 23–24.

Gumballs in a Jar
Curriculum Topic Study
Related CTS Guide: Probability

STUDENT RESPONSES TO "GUMBALLS IN A JAR"

Sample Responses: C

Student 1: Jar A and Jar B have the same chance because one has 3 and 2 and one has 6 and 4 so it would be the same chance because for every 2 white gumballs there are 3 black gumballs.

Student 2: They are the same; just Jar B is doubled so chance is still the same.

Student 3: I think C because in each jar there are more black gumballs than white gumballs so therefore I think that you would pull out a black gumball [rather] than a white gumball.

Student 4: Because there are more black gumballs in each jar.

Sample Responses: A

Student 5: Even though Jar B has more black gumballs, A has only 2 white gumballs so A has a better chance of picking a black gumball.

Student 6: Jar A has a 3 to 2 ratio (3 black to 2 white). Jar B has a 5 to 5 ratio (50%).

Sample Responses: B

Student 7: I selected B because there is a greater percentage of black to white gumballs; therefore having a higher probability.

Student 8: Jar B has more black gumballs.

VARIATION: GUMBALLS IN A JAR II

Choose the most accurate statement.

A. There is a better chance of getting a black gumball from the jar.

B. There is a better chance of getting a white gumball from the jar.

C. There is an equal chance of getting a white or black gumball.

Explain your reason for the statement you selected.

_____

_____

_____

_____

_____

_____

_____

_____

_____

VARIATION: GUMBALLS IN A JAR III

Jar A: 4 white gumballs and 6 black gumballs

Jar B: 6 white gumballs and 9 black gumballs

Jar A   **Jar B**

Which statement best describes the chance of getting a *black* gumball?

A. There is a better chance of getting a black gumball from Jar A.

B. There is a better chance of getting a black gumball from Jar B.

C. The chance of getting a black gumball is the same for both Jar A and Jar B.

Explain your reason(s) for the statement you selected.

_____

_____

_____

_____

_____

_____

_____

THE SPINNERS

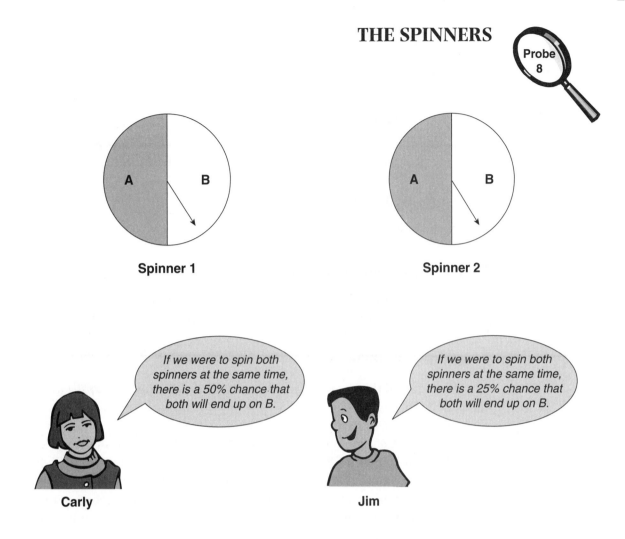

Who do you agree with? Explain your thinking.

TEACHERS' NOTES: THE SPINNERS

Grade Level for "The Spinners" Probe

Grades K–2	3–5	6–8	9–12
			▓▓▓

*Q*uestioning for Student Understanding

Are students able to apply the concepts of compound probability?

*U*ncovering Understandings

The Spinners Content Standard: Data Analysis and Probability
Variation: Commuting to Work (may uncover the "conjunction fallacy."

*E*xamining Student Work

The distracter, there is a 50% chance, may reveal a *common error* regarding compound probability.

- *The correct answer is a 25% chance.* The possible outcomes are AA, BB, AB, and BA, with BB as 1 out of 4. The majority of the students who answered correctly used the approach of multiplying the probability of the first spinner landing on B and the probability of the second spinner landing on B. Fewer students listed the possible outcomes to find the answer. (See Students 1, 2, and 3 in *Student Responses* section.)
- *Distracter 50% chance.* Some students incorrectly reason that because each spinner has a 50% chance of landing on B, there is also a 50% chance for both to land on B. Other students incorrectly choose 50% because there are two B sections out of four total sections. (See Students 4, 5, and 6 in *Student Responses* section.)

*S*eeking Links to Cognitive Research

In their studies, Tversky and Kahneman found that tertiary level students exhibit conjunction fallacy-thinking that compound events are more likely to occur than simple events. (NCTM, 2003 p. 221)

[The NAEP data on a similar item] indicates that students' difficulties with conjunctions are more than just psychological. Students lacked the mathematical skills to analyze or list the outcomes for the spinner problem. (NCTM, 2003, p. 222)

After initial difficulties with the spinner problem, students who were made cognizant of listing the sample space and who analyzed data collected from a number of trials were more likely to change their thinking. (Shaughnessy & Ciancetta, 2002)

Teaching Implications

To support a deeper understanding for students in high school in regard to probability, the following are ideas and questions to consider in conjunction with the research.

Focus Through Instruction

- Help students construct sample spaces and distributions
- Give students experience listing the set of all possible outcomes in probability experiments
- Provide multiple opportunities in using or collecting actual data, making and testing conjectures, and communicating their findings to fellow classmates
- Use computer simulations to enable students to investigate more realistic situations than were previously possible

Questions to Consider . . . *when working with students as they grapple with the idea of probability*

- Are students making use of sample spaces when predicting expected results?
- Are students able to calculate expected values?
- Do students understand that when two events can occur separately or together, the conjunction cannot be more likely than the likelihood of either of the two individual events?

Teacher Sound Bite

"In the past, I spent very little time on sample space and experiments since I felt students had this experience prior to high school and could now move toward a calculation approach. Examining my students' work on this probe, reading the research and teaching suggestions, and talking with others has changed my view of teaching compound probability. My most important insight was to allow students to make predictions first and then allow them to figure out ways to test their predictions. This has changed my approach to teaching probability."

Additional References for Research and Teaching Implications

Lee (1999), *Resources for Teaching and Learning about Probability and Statistics.*

NCTM (1993b), *Research Ideas for the Classroom: High School Mathematics,* pp. 177–194.

NCTM (2000). *Principles and Standards for School Mathematics,* pp. 324, 331–333.

NCTM (2003), *Research Companion to the Principles and Standards for School Mathematics,* pp. 222, 224.

Shaughnessy & Ciancetta (2002), *Students' Understanding of the Variability in a Probability Environment.*

The Spinners

Curriculum Topic Study

Related CTS Guide:
Probability

STUDENT RESPONSES TO "THE SPINNERS"

Sample Responses: 25%

Student 1: I think Jim is correct since it can't be 50%. It should be ½ of 50% since both spinners are 50%.

Student 2: I agree with Jim. You multiply ½ × ½ to solve this type of problem.

Student 3: It has to be Jim. Just list the possible outcomes and look for what you want. We want BB, which is supposed to happen 25% of the time. This may not be true if we actually tried it out, but it is just in theory.

First Spinner	Second Spinner
A	A
A	B
B	B
B	A

Sample Responses: 50%

Student 4: Carly is right since there are 2 Bs out of 4 possible spaces (2 As and 2 Bs).

Student 5: I agree with Carly since there is 50% chance of landing on B for each spinner.

Student 6: To find probability, you put number of successes over possible outcomes. Carly is correct since 2/4 is the same as 50%.

VARIATION: **COMMUTING TO WORK**

On a given day, all the people who commute to work in a large city are monitored. Which is more likely to occur?

    A. A person has an automobile accident.

    B. A person has an automobile accident and is under 21 years of age.

    Explain your choice.

_____

_____

_____

_____

_____

_____

_____

_____

_____

5

Geometry and Measurement Assessment Probes

Key

	Target for Instruction Based on National Standards and Cognitive Research
	Prerequisite Concept/Field Testing Indicates Student Difficulty

Question	Probe	Grade Span Bars			
		K–2	3–5	6–8	9–12
Chapter 5: Geometry and Measurement					
What do students understand about the attributes of a triangle?	What Does a Triangle Look Like?				
What do students understand about properties of a rectangle and their relationship to a square?	What Does a Rectangle Look Like?				
What do students understand and not understand about linear measurement?	How Long Is the Pencil?				
Do students perceive the length of an angle's rays as having an effect on the angle's measure?	Comparing Angles				
Do students accurately compare the volume and surface area of a box before and after dividing it into four boxes?	Box Cutting/ Comparing Volume and Surface Area				
Are students familiar with the attributes of parallelograms?	Parallelograms				
Do students understand how to find the volume of a box, given the side lengths or given the area of a face and the length of the other side?	Volume of a Box				

135

WHAT DOES A TRIANGLE LOOK LIKE?

Circle all the figures that are triangles.

A.

B.

C.

D.

E.

F.

G.

Explain why each figure you circled is a triangle.

_____

_____

_____

_____

_____

_____

_____

TEACHERS' NOTES: WHAT DOES A TRIANGLE LOOK LIKE?

Grade Level for "What Does a Triangle Look Like?" Probe

Grades K–2	3–5	6–8	9–12

Questioning for Student Understanding

What do students understand about the attributes of a triangle?

Uncovering Understandings

What Does a Triangle Look Like? Content Standard: Geometry

Examining Student Work

The distracters may reveal *overgeneralizations* made by students as they base decisions on a single attribute or property in identifying a triangle.

- *The correct answers are A, D, and G.* A, D, and G are examples of triangles. Students who indicate these and not the nonexamples have a working definition that includes nonstandard orientation of the figure—that is, sideways, upside down, and so on—as they identify the attributes of a triangle successfully. (See Students 5 and 6 in *Student Responses* section.)
- *Students who answer A, C, D and G.* Students who indicate A, C, D, and G applied their working definition of a triangle as being three sides and three points or corners. Because they add C to the group, it appears that they do not realize that an important attribute of a triangle is straight lines. (See Students 1 and 2 in *Student Responses* section.)
- *Students who answer A, D, E, and G.* Students who indicate A, D, E, and G used the idea of three lines and three points and decided to add E as an almost or "without a bottom" triangle. Many students extended the lines to close E, which would then be a triangle. However, being a closed figure is a necessary attribute of triangles, which students must understand. (See Students 3 and 4 in *Student Responses* section.)

Seeking Links to Cognitive Research

Children generally enter school with a great deal of knowledge about shapes. They can identify circles quite accurately and squares fairly well as early as age four. They are less accurate at recognizing triangles (about 60% correct) and rectangles (about 50% correct). Given conventional instruction, which tends to elicit and verify this prior knowledge, children generally fail to make much improvement in their knowledge of shapes from preschool through the elementary grades. (NRC, 2001, p. 284)

Children begin forming concepts of shape long before formal schooling. The primary grades are an ideal time to help them refine and extend their understandings. Students first learn to recognize a shape by its appearance as a whole or through qualities such as "pointiness." They may believe that a given figure is a rectangle because "it looks like a door." (NCTM, 2000, p. 39)

Very young children can learn rich concepts about shape if provided with varied examples and non-examples, discussions about shapes and their characteristics, and interesting tasks. Research indicates that curricula should ensure that children experience many different examples of a type of shape. For example, showing a rich variety of triangles and distracters that would be sure to generate discussion. Showing non-examples that when compared to similar examples, help focus attention on the critical attributes. (Clements & Sarama, 2004, p. 285)

In grades K–2: Schools should provide sufficient opportunities for children to learn about geometric figures. By the end of second grade they should be able to "identify a wide range of examples and non-examples of a wide range of geometric figures; classify, describe, draw and visualize shapes; and describe and compare shapes based on their attributes." (NRC, 2001, p. 285)

In the early grades, students will have classified and sorted geometric objects such as triangles or cylinders by noting general characteristics. Students in grades 3–5 should develop more precise ways to describe shapes, focusing on identifying and describing the shape's properties and learning specialized vocabulary associated with these shapes and properties. To consolidate their ideas, students should draw and construct shapes, compare and discuss their attributes, classify them, and develop and consider definitions on the basis of a shape's properties, such as that a rectangle has four straight sides and four square corner[s]. (NCTM, 2000, p. 161)

*T*eaching Implications

To support a deeper understanding for students in elementary school in regard to geometry, specifically attributes of triangles, the following are ideas and questions to consider in conjunction with the research.

Focus Through Instruction

- Teachers need to provide materials and structure the environment appropriately to encourage students to explore shapes and their attributes

- Students should analyze characteristics and properties of two- and three-dimensional geometric shapes
- Teachers should ensure that students see geometric shapes and sort them by looking at examples and nonexamples
- Students should engage in mathematical conjectures about geometric relationships
- Students should be exposed to and expected to use appropriate terminology
- Students need experiences with combining or cutting apart shapes to form new shapes
- Teachers need to provide opportunities for students to sort, build, draw, model, trace, measure, and construct the ability to visualize geometric relationships
- By Grades 3 through 5, students should begin to develop more precise ways to describe shapes by focusing on identifying and describing the shape's properties

Questions to Consider . . . *when working with students as they grapple with these ideas of attributes of shapes*

- Do students begin to identify shapes by geometric attributes?
- Do students apply the same definition of a triangle, even if the position or orientation is "upside down" or unfamiliar?
- Are students using mathematical language to describe shapes?
- When students combine shapes or cut apart shapes to form new shapes, do they display them in varying positions?

Teacher Sound Bite

"I realize now that I have made assumptions about what my students know about triangles. Much of what they understand is derived from seeing equilateral triangles. It is important for me to introduce students to both examples and nonexamples through instruction and activities."

Additional References for Research and Teaching Implications

Clements & Sarama (2004), *Engaging Young Children in Mathematics*, pp. 267–292.
NCTM (1993a), *Research Ideas for the Classroom: Early Childhood Mathematics*, pp. 195–220.
NCTM (2000), *Principles and Standards for School Mathematics*, pp. 39, 161.
NCTM (2006b), *Teachers Engaged in Research*, pp. 153–169.
NRC (2001), *Adding It Up: Helping Children Learn Mathematics*, pp. 284–285.

What Does a Triangle Look Like?
Curriculum Topic Study
Related CTS Guide: Triangles

STUDENT RESPONSES TO "WHAT DOES A TRIANGLE LOOK LIKE?"

Sample A, C, D, and G Responses

Student 1: I only circled the ones that had three sides because triangles only have three sides.

Student 2: I chose A, C, D, and G because they have three corners.

Sample A, D, E, and G Responses

Student 3: Because all have three sides. A looks like a triangle. D looks like a long triangle. E looks like a triangle with no point. G looks like a sideways triangle.

Student 4: A looks like a triangle. D is a longer triangle. E is a triangle without a bottom. G is a triangle kind of upside down.

Sample A, D and G Responses

Student 5: I chose A because I know it's a triangle because it's the most common triangle. I chose D because it has three points. I chose G because it looks like A, and it also has three tips.

Student 6: I know that triangles have three lines and three points and the lines are all straight.

WHAT DOES A RECTANGLE LOOK LIKE?

Circle all the figures that are rectangles.

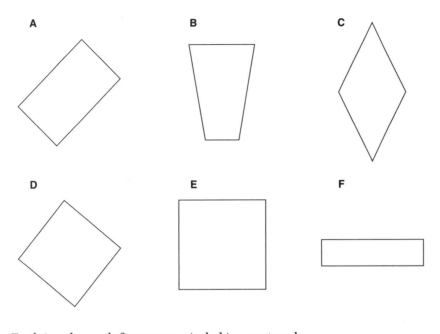

Explain why each figure you circled is a rectangle.

_____

_____

_____

_____

_____

_____

_____

TEACHERS' NOTES: WHAT DOES A RECTANGLE LOOK LIKE?

Grade Level for "What Does a Rectangle Look Like?" Probe

Grades K–2	3–5	6–8	9–12

Questioning for Student Understanding

What do students understand about properties of a rectangle and their relationship to a square?

Uncovering Understandings

What Does a Rectangle Look Like? Content Standard: Geometry

Examining Student Work

The distracters may reveal *overgeneralizations* made by students as they make decisions classifying shapes based on a single attribute or property when identifying rectangles.

- *The correct answers are A, D, E, and F.* The rectangles are identified correctly using the working definition of a rectangle as a figure with four sides and four right angles. (See Students 5 and 6 in *Student Responses* section.)
- *Students who answer A, D, and E.* Students who choose A, D, and E undergeneralized their understanding of a rectangle by not extending their definition to apply to F. (See Students 1 and 2 in *Student Responses* section.)
- *Students who answer B and C.* Students who choose B and C applied the properties of a four-sided figure with four angles without considering the attribute of four *right* angles. (See Students 3 and 4 in *Student Responses* section.)

Seeking Links to Cognitive Research

Children generally enter school with a great deal of knowledge about shapes. They can identify circles quite accurately and squares fairly well as early as age four. They are less accurate at recognizing triangles (about 60% correct) and rectangles (about 50% correct). Given conventional instruction, which tends to elicit and verify this prior knowledge, children generally fail to make much improvement in their knowledge of shapes from preschool through the elementary grades. (NRC, 2001, p. 284)

Children begin forming concepts of shape long before formal schooling. The primary grades are an ideal time to help them refine and extend their understandings. Students first learn to recognize a shape by its appearance as a whole or through qualities such as "pointiness." They may believe that a given figure is a rectangle because "it looks like a door." (NCTM, 2000, p. 39)

Very young children can learn rich concepts about shape if provided with varied examples and non-examples, discussions about shapes and their characteristics, and interesting tasks. Research indicates that curricula should ensure that children experience many different examples of a type of shape. For example, showing a rich variety of triangles and distracters that would be sure to generate discussion. Showing non-examples that compared to similar examples, help focus attention on the critical attributes. (Clements & Sarama, 2004, p. 285)

In grades K–2: Schools should provide sufficient opportunities for children to learn about geometric figures. By the end of second grade they should be able to "identify a wide range of examples and non-examples of a wide range of geometric figures; classify, describe, draw and visualize shapes; and describe and compare shapes based on their attributes." (NRC, 2001, p. 285)

In the early grades, students will have classified and sorted geometric objects such as triangles or cylinders by noting general characteristics. Students in grades 3–5 should develop more precise ways to describe shapes, focusing on identifying and describing the shape's properties and learning specialized vocabulary associated with these shapes and properties. To consolidate their ideas, students should draw and construct shapes, compare and discuss their attributes, classify them, and develop and consider definitions on the basis of a shape's properties, such as that a rectangle has four straight sides and four square corner. (NCTM, 2000, p. 161)

*T*eaching Implications

To support a deeper understanding for students in elementary school in regard to rectangles, the following are ideas and questions to consider in conjunction with the research.

Focus Through Instruction

- Teachers need to provide materials and structure the environment appropriately to encourage students to explore shapes and their attributes
- Students should analyze characteristics and properties of two- and three-dimensional shapes
- Teachers should ensure that students see geometric shapes and sort them by looking at examples and nonexamples of rectangles

- Students should engage in mathematical conjectures about geometric relationships to consider why a square is a rectangle but a rectangle is not always a square
- Students should develop more precise ways to describe shapes using specialized vocabulary associated with rectangles and squares
- Teachers need to provide opportunities for students to sort, build, draw, model, trace, measure, and construct the ability to visualize geometric relationships and verbalize observations

Questions to Consider . . . *when working with students as they grapple with these ideas of attributes of rectangles*

- Do students begin to identify shapes by using the geometric attributes/properties of those shapes?
- Do students apply the same definition of a rectangle even if the position or orientation is unfamiliar or the shape is a square?
- Are students using mathematical language to describe rectangles and address the similarities and differences of rectangles and squares?

Teacher Sound Bite

"Students consistently seem to struggle with answering the question, If a square is a rectangle, why isn't a rectangle a square? Having students articulate their thinking from this probe has given me invaluable information to be able to address this idea for all of my students other than just to state the relationship."

Additional References for Research and Teaching Implications

What Does a Rectangle Look Like?
Curriculum Topic Study
Related CTS Guide: Quadrilaterals

Clements & Sarama (2004), *Engaging Young Children in Mathematics*, pp. 285, 267–292.

NCTM (1993a), *Research Ideas for the Classroom: Early Childhood Mathematics*, pp. 195–220.

NCTM (2000), *Principles and Standards for School Mathematics*, pp. 39, 161.

NRC (2001), *Adding It Up: Helping Children Learn Mathematics*, pp. 284–285.

STUDENT RESPONSES TO "WHAT DOES A RECTANGLE LOOK LIKE?"

Sample A, D, and E Responses

Student 1: I know that rectangles have four sides and four lines like a square.

Student 2: I chose the shapes that look like long squares.

Sample B and C Responses

Student 3: I think that B and C are rectangles because they are just stretched out.

Student 4: I know that four sides and four corners make a rectangle.

Sample A, D, E, and F Responses

Student 5: I picked A, D, E, and F because they all have four sides and four corners and the sides are parallel lines across from each other.

Student 6: I know that they are rectangles because they have four sides which are two pairs of parallel lines and have four straight corners.

HOW LONG IS THE PENCIL?

Are any of the pencils the same length?

A	B

0 1 2 3 4 5   0 1 2 3 4 5 6

C	D

0 1 2 3 4 5   0 1 2 3 4 5 6

How do you know if any of the pencils are the same length?

_____

_____

_____

_____

_____

_____

_____

_____

_____

TEACHERS' NOTES: HOW LONG IS THE PENCIL?

Grade Level for "How Long Is the Pencil?" Probe

Grades K–2	3–5	6–8	9–12

*Q*uestioning for Student Understanding

What do students understand and not understand about linear measurement?

*U*ncovering Understandings

How Long Is the Pencil? Content Standard: Measurement
Variation: How Long Is the String?

*E*xamining Student Work

The distracters may reveal *common errors* regarding linear measurement such as not responding to nonzero origins by reading off the number that aligns with the end of the object.

- *The correct answer is Yes, A and B are of equal length.* The measurement for both pencils is 5 inches. In A, the tip of the pencil aligns with the end of the ruler, which is not the starting point for accurate measuring. In B, the tip of the pencil aligns with the 0 point with the eraser ending at the 5-inch mark. To reconcile the measurements, students must adjust Pencil A to begin at the 0 point, in which case, the eraser will end at the 5-inch mark. (See Students 5 and 6 in *Student Responses* section.)
- *Students who answer B and C as equal.* Students who choose B and C most likely looked at the eraser of the pencil and judged that they both measured 5 inches. Their error is not considering the beginning point on the ruler as it relates to the beginning of the object being measured. (See Students 1 and 2 in *Student Responses* section.)
- *Students who answer A and D as equal.* Students who choose A and D most likely considered the inch difference in D but failed to recognize that Pencil A did not begin at zero, thus making the pencils not an equal length. (See Students 3 and 4 in *Student Responses* section.)

*S*eeking Links to Cognitive Research

Students focused on one end of the line and read the number off the ruler in the same manner that you would read a thermometer. Students missed the importance of the starting place in positioning the ruler. We need to emphasize the role of the ruler as an aid for counting units. If you begin at 0, the number on the ruler coincides with the count of units, but it is just as important to realize that you can begin anywhere and use the scale on the ruler to help count the number of units in the length. (NCTM, 1993a, pp. 181–182)

Children's understanding of zero-point is particularly tenuous. Only a minority of young children understand that any point on a scale can serve as the starting point, and even a significant minority of older children (e.g., fifth grade) respond to nonzero origins by simply reading off whatever number on a ruler aligns with the end of the object (Lehrer et al., 1998a). Many children throughout schooling begin measuring with one rather than zero (Ellis, Siegler, & Van Voorhis, 2001). (NCTM, 2003, p. 183)

Further work in classrooms suggests the importance of providing opportunities for children to repeatedly "split" (Confrey, 1995; Confrey & Smith, 1995), or partition, lengths to come to understand unit partitions. For example, in second-grade classrooms where students had the opportunity to design rulers, students were motivated by their previous experience with rulers to add "marks" that would help them measure lengths that were parts of units, for instance 3 and ½. (NCTM, 2003, pp. 183–184)

In grades K–2, students develop measurement concepts and skills as they position multiple copies of the same units without leaving spaces between them or as they measure by iterating one unit without overlapping or leaving gaps. Both types of experiences are necessary. Similarly, using rulers, students learn concepts and procedures, including accurate alignment (e.g., ignoring the leading edge at the beginning of many rulers), starting at zero, and focusing on the lengths of the units rather than only on the numbers on the ruler. (NCTM, 2000, p. 106)

In grades 3–5, an expanded number of tools and range of measurement techniques should be available to students. When using conventional tools such as rulers and tape measures for measuring length, students will need instruction to learn to use these tools properly. For example, they will need to recognize and understand the markings on a ruler, including where the "0," or beginning point, is located. (NCTM, 2000, p. 173)

*T*eaching Implications

To support a deeper understanding for students in elementary school in regard to measurement, the following are ideas and questions to consider in conjunction with the research.

Focus Through Instruction

- Have students develop a ruler of their own, revealing their current level of understanding of rulers
- Help students recognize the importance of units by working with identical units and the role of standard units in measurement (e.g., paper clips of same size, feet of same size)
- Have students count units so they begin to make sense of iteration (reusing units, e.g., no space in between objects lined up to be measured/counted)
- Help students explore measurement with a variety of units, nonstandard as well as standard, to develop their understanding of units
- Give students practice with partitioning units (i.e., units being measured may not be a whole unit; therefore, dividing units by 1/2 and so on is an important connection)
- Encourage students to focus on the importance of the zero point of the tool or units and the end point of the object being measured as a relationship
- Use estimation activities to help students focus on attributes being measured, the process of measuring, the sizes of units, and the value of referents
- Provide experiences that help students get a "sense of" what units look like as they build an internal idea of lengths (e.g., centimeters, inches, feet, yards, meters, etc.)

Questions to Consider . . . *when working with students as they grapple with these ideas of measurement*

- Do they line objects up to be measured, leaving no spaces in between objects?
- Do they recognize that objects of varying size impact the results?
- When they begin to measure or count, where do they start? finish?
- What do students do with any left-over space?
- Are their estimates in the ball park of the unit or tool they choose to use?

Teacher Sound Bite

"I never even thought to look at rulers to see where the starting point was. I am going to be purposeful about making it explicit to students and also have students consider why it is important to look at the starting point when they measure."

How Long Is the Pencil?
Curriculum Topic Study
Related CTS Guide: Length

Additional References for Research and Teaching Implications

NCTM (1993a), *Research Ideas for the Classroom: Early Childhood Mathematics*, pp. 181–182.

NCTM (1993c), *Research Ideas for the Classroom: Middle Grades Mathematics*, pp. 79–80.

NCTM (2000), *Principles and Standards for School Mathematics*, pp. 106, 173.

NCTM (2003), *Research Companion to Principles and Standards for School Mathematics*, pp. 182–184.

NCTM (2006b), *Teachers Engaged in Research*, pp. 109–133.

STUDENT RESPONSES TO "HOW LONG IS THE PENCIL?"

Sample B and C Responses

Student 1: Because I put lines on the ends of the pencils, and it led to a part on the ruler which equaled an amount. B and C had the same amount.

Student 2: Yes, B and C are the same by the length they are, both right on the 5.

Sample A and D Responses

Student 3: Yes, because A is measured out right and says 4 1/2 inches but D is not measured right so is not 5 and 1/2. It is 4 and 1/2 because it starts on 1.

Student 4: Well, since they don't start at the same place, I just add up the inches.

Sample A and B Responses

Student 5: Because A goes from the end of the ruler to 4 1/2 inches. Then B is past it at 5 inches but starts at half of an inch and so if A is moved to the zero it would measure 5 inches just like B.

Student 6: A and B are the same because even though A only goes to 4 1/2 and B goes all the way to the 5 mark, they are still the same because on A there is only a half an inch between point and zero so 4 1/2 plus 1/2 equals 5. So A and B are the same.

VARIATION: HOW LONG IS THE STRING?

Probe
3a

Which string is longer?

A _____

B _____

C _____

How do you know?

_____

_____

_____

_____

_____

_____

_____

_____

COMPARING ANGLES

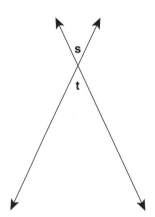

Examine the figure above. In this figure, two straight lines intersect at a point. Read the statements below about angles *s* and *t*. Circle the statement that best describes the relationship between the two angles.

A. The measure of angle *s* is bigger than the measure of angle *t*.

B. The measure of angle *t* is bigger than the measure of angle *s*.

C. Angle *s* and angle *t* have the same measure.

Describe the rule you used to decide the relationship between the two angles. If you wish, include a picture or example to explain your idea.

_____

_____

_____

_____

_____

_____

_____

_____

TEACHERS' NOTES: COMPARING ANGLES

Grade Level for "Comparing Angles" Probe

Grades K–2	3–5	6–8	9–12

Questioning for Student Understanding

Do students perceive the length of an angle's rays as having an effect on the angle's measure?

Uncovering Understandings

Comparing Angles Content Standards: Geometry and Measurement
Variations: Comparing Angles II, Comparing Angles III (arc at different distance to vertex), and Comparing Angles IV (arc at different distance to vertex)

Examining Student Work

The distracters may reveal *common errors* reflecting the intuitive rule of "more A means more B" (Stavy & Tirosh, 2000, pp. 4–8). Students perceive the measure of the angles to be dependent on the lengths of the rays that make the sides of the angles.

- *The correct response is C.* Angles *s* and *t* are vertical angles and have the same measure. The lengths of the angles' rays do not affect angle measure. (See Students 1 and 2 in *Student Responses* section.)
- *Distracter A.* Students generally do not choose angle *s* as it does not appear to be bigger than angle *t*.
- *Distracter B:* Students who choose B typically see more space (area) in the figure at angle *t* because the rays are extended further. Students sometimes do not realize that rays are continuous and can be extended as far as one would like to draw. This is sometimes called the intuitive rule of "more A means more B," which in this case would correspond to longer ray length means greater angle measure. (See Student 3, 4 and 5 in *Student Responses* section.)

Seeking Links to Cognitive Research

Students hold many different schemes regarding not only the angle concept but also the size of angles. They frequently relate the size of an angle to the length of the line segments that form its sides, the tilt of the top line segment, the area enclosed by the triangular region defined by the drawn sides, the length between the sides, the proximity of the two sides, or the turn at the vertex (Clements & Battista, 1989). (NCTM, 2003, p. 163)

*T*eaching Implications

To support a deeper understanding for students in middle school in regard to angle measurement, the following are ideas and questions to consider in conjunction with the research.

Focus Through Instruction

- The study of geometry in Grades 3 through 5 requires thinking *and* doing; as students sort, build, draw, model, trace, measure, and construct, their capacity to visualize geometric relationships will develop
- In middle grades, students should investigate relationships by drawing, measuring, visualizing, comparing, transforming, and classifying geometric objects
- Students should be actively engaged with geometric ideas using concrete models, drawings, geoboards, dot paper, multiple-length cardboard strips with hinges, and dynamic geometry software
- With well-designed activities, appropriate tools, and teachers' support, students can make and explore conjectures about geometry and can learn to reason carefully about geometric ideas
- Students need to encounter multiple mathematical conceptions of angle, including (a) angle as movement, as in rotation or sweep; (b) angle as a geometric shape, a delineation of space by two intersecting lines; and (c) angle as a measure, a perspective that encompasses the other two.

Questions to Consider . . . *when working with students as they grapple with the idea of angle measurement*

- Can students identify vertical angles?
- Do students apply the definition of congruent angles to various shapes and sizes?
- Can students accurately recognize geometric labeling and symbols?
- Do student look at the size of angles' rays as a way to compare angle measure?

Teacher Sound Bite

"I was very surprised that my students incorrectly chose B. We spent considerable time discussing the relationship between vertical angles. In the future, I will need to make sure that my students have more hands-on experiences with angles and also make sure my drawings of vertical angles are not always with the same ray length."

Additional References for Research and Teaching Implications

AAAS (1993), *Benchmarks for Science Literacy*, pp. 223–224, 352, 360.

NCTM (2000), *Principles and Standards for School Mathematics*, pp. 41–42, 43, 44, 165–166, 171–172, 233–234, 243.

NCTM (2002), *Reflecting on NCTM's Principles and Standards in Elementary and Middle School Mathematics*, pp. 164–169.

NCTM (2003), *Research Companion to Principles and Standards for School Mathematics*, pp. 152–155, 162–164, 187.

NRC (2001), *Adding It Up: Helping Children Learn Mathematics*, pp. 284–286.

Stavy & Tirosh (2000), *How Students (Mis-)Understand Science and Mathematics*, pp. 1–9.

Comparing Angles
Curriculum Topic Study
Related CTS Guide: Angle Measurement and Geometric Relationships

STUDENT RESPONSES TO "COMPARING ANGLES"

Sample Responses: C

Student 1: Vertical angles are congruent.

Student 2: When two lines cross, they form angles that are the same.

Sample Responses: B

Student 3: Angle *t* is further spread. It looks to be about a 45° angle while angle *s* is closer together and looks about a 30° angle. The lines had a further distance to travel before making angle *t,* and that is why it is a bigger angle.

Student 4: Because angle *t* has a lot more space than angle *s* does. The angles and the sides are bigger in angle *t* than in angle *s*.

Student 5: I chose B because I knew it was an obtuse angle, while *s* was acute, so B is correct since obtuse angles are bigger than acute angles.

VARIATION: COMPARING ANGLES II

Examine the figures. Read the statements below about angles *s* and *t*. Circle the statement that best describes the relationship between the two angles.

A. The measure of angle *s* is bigger than the measure of angle *t*.

B. The measure of angle *t* is bigger than the measure of angle *s*.

C. Angle *s* and angle *t* have the same measure.

Describe the rule you used to decide the relationship between the two angles. If you wish, include a picture or example to explain your idea.

_____

_____

_____

_____

_____

_____

_____

_____

_____

_____

VARIATION: COMPARING ANGLES III

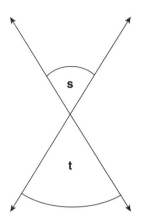

Examine the figure above. In this figure, two straight lines intersect at a point. Read the statements below about the angles *s* and *t*. Circle the statement that best describes the relationship between the two angles.

A. The measure of angle *s* is bigger than the measure of angle *t*.

B. The measure of angle *t* is bigger than the measure of angle *s*.

C. Angle *s* and angle *t* have the same measure.

Describe the rule you used to decide the relationship between the two angles. If you wish, include a picture or example to explain your idea.

_____

_____

_____

_____

_____

_____

_____

_____

VARIATION: COMPARING ANGLES IV

Examine the figures above. Read the statements below about the angles *s* and *t*. Circle the statement that best describes the relationship between the two angles.

A. The measure of angle *s* is bigger than the measure of angle *t*.

B. The measure of angle *t* is bigger than the measure of angle *s*.

C. Angle *s* and angle *t* have the same measure.

Describe the rule you used to decide the relationship between the angles. If you wish, include a picture or example to explain your idea.

_____

_____

_____

_____

_____

_____

_____

_____

_____

BOX CUTTING/COMPARING VOLUME AND SURFACE AREA

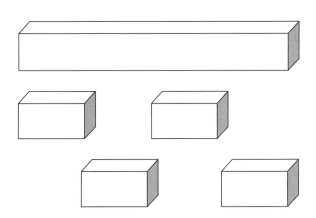

Look at the boxes above. Imagine that the long box at the top has been divided into four pieces, making the four boxes shown underneath. Circle each statement that you agree with.

A. The volume of the undivided box is greater than the total volumes of the divided boxes.

B. The volume of the undivided box is less than the total volumes of the divided boxes.

C. The volume of the undivided box is equal to the total volumes of the divided boxes.

D. The surface area of the undivided box is greater than the total surface areas of the divided boxes.

E. The surface area of the undivided box is less than the total surface areas of the divided boxes.

F. The surface area of the undivided box is equal to the total surface areas of the divided boxes.

Describe the process you used to help you select the response(s) from the list above.

TEACHERS' NOTES: BOX CUTTING/COMPARING VOLUME AND SURFACE AREA

Grade Level for "Box Cutting/Comparing Volume and Surface Area" Probe

Grades K–2	3–5	6–8	9–12

*Q*uestioning for Student Understanding

Do students accurately compare the volume and surface area of a box before and after dividing it into four boxes?

*U*ncovering Understandings

Box Cutting Content Standard: Measurement

*E*xamining Student Work

The distracters may reveal *common errors* such as the intuitive rule of "same A means same B" (Stavy & Tirosh, 2000, p. 56) or a student's lack of *conceptual* understanding of surface area and volume.

- *The correct responses are C and E.* The volume of the long box is the same as the volume of the four smaller boxes. Although volume is preserved, surface area is not. The surface area of the four smaller boxes is greater than the longer box as it has several more sides. (See Student 1 in *Student Responses* section.)
- *Distracter A.* Students who choose A typically see the sides of the smaller boxes as taking up space. Although this is true to a small extent, it does not change volume drastically. Students who have this trend in thinking might very well be on the right track conceptually, especially if they realized that the surface area increases with the divided boxes. (See Student 2 in *Student Responses* section.)
- *Distracter B.* This is generally not a trend in student thinking but is placed in the probe to complete all the choices.
- *Distracter D.* This is also not typically a trend, but some students see surface area being lost when the box is divided. (See Student 3 in *Student Responses* section.)
- *Distracter F.* This is the most common trend in incorrect thinking. Students think that volume and surface area are preserved in the dividing. This is an intuitive rule of Same A means Same B. In this case, it is transferred as preserving volume means preserving surface area. (See Students 4, 5, and 6 in *Student Responses* section.)

Seeking Links to Cognitive Research

Students use the intuitive rule of "Same A infers Same B" when thinking about volume and surface area of a box and its divided parts. (Stavy & Tirosh, 2000, pp. 56–57)

Teaching Implications

To support a deeper understanding for students in middle school in regard to volume and surface area, the following are ideas and questions to consider in conjunction with the research.

Focus Through Instruction

- As they progress through school, not only should students' repertoire of measurable attributes expand, but their understanding of the relationships between attributes should also develop
- Students should explore how the surface area of a rectangular prism can vary as the volume is held constant
- Students in the middle grades should develop formulas for the volume and surface area of objects; they should have opportunities to see the connections between the formula and the actual object
- Frequent hands-on experiences in measuring surface area and volume can help students develop a sound understanding of the relationships among attributes

Questions to Consider . . . *when working with students as they grapple with the ideas of volume and surface area*

- Do students have a conceptual understanding of surface area and volume?
- Can students communicate what information is needed to find volume and surface area of objects?
- Have students developed strategies to determine volume and surface area of different shaped objects?
- Do students see volume and surface area as being connected when change in an object's attributes occurs?

Teacher Sound Bite

"I was very interested to learn that my students thought that the surface area would not change when the box was cut up. We will be doing some hands-on investigations tomorrow!"

Box Cutting/ Comparing Volume and Surface Area *Curriculum Topic Study* Related CTS Guide: Perimeter, Area and Volume

Additional References for Research and Teaching Implications

AAAS (1993), *Benchmarks for Science Literacy*, pp. 222–225, 352.

NCTM (2000), *Principles and Standards for School Mathematics*, pp. 41, 44–46, 172–175, 241–245.

Stavy & Tirosh (2000), *How Students (Mis-)Understand Science and Mathematics*, pp. 50–57.

STUDENT RESPONSES TO "BOX CUTTING/ COMPARING VOLUME AND SURFACE AREA"

Sample Response: CE

Student 1: The divided boxes still hold the same amount of space as the one large one. The surface area is different because there are six extra sides in the divided boxes.

Sample Response: A

Student 2: The box being divided into four smaller ones is going to make the volume be less. The single box has more volume because it doesn't have the sides blocking any space. There is more surface area on the four smaller boxes. The four boxes have more area on the surface because they have more sides to be counted.

Sample Response: D

Student 3: I picked D because the surface area was lost when you divide the box. If you divide the box, you lose surface area.

Sample Responses: F

Student 4: The smaller boxes put together are the same size as the whole box so there would not be any difference. They both take up the same amount of volume and same amount of surface area.

Student 5: The description said to just divide the box so that all the smaller cubes together are going to be the exact same as the big box.

Student 6: I determined that if it's the same box but just divided up into different pieces, then it would have the same dimensions. Therefore, the volume of the separate blocks would be equal to the original box. The surface area of the blocks would also be equal to the original.

PARALLELOGRAMS

Probe
6

Circle the figures that are parallelograms.

A.

B.

C.

D.

E.

F.

G.

H.

75°

75°

Explain your reasoning for each figure.

A.

_____

_____

B.

_____

_____

C.

_____

_____

D.

_____

_____

E.

_____

_____

F.

_____

_____

G.

_____

_____

H.

_____

_____

TEACHERS' NOTES: PARALLELOGRAMS

Grade Level for "Parallelograms" Probe

Grades K–2	3–5	6–8	9–12

*Q*uestioning for Student Understanding

Are students familiar with the attributes of parallelograms?

*U*ncovering Understandings

Parallelograms Content Standard: Geometry

*E*xamining Student Work

The distracters may reveal *common errors* in assumptions students have about information given (or not given) in geometric figures or a lack in *conceptual knowledge* about properties of angles, parallel lines, and/or parallelograms.

- *The correct responses are B and H.* Parallelograms are a special type of quadrilateral. A quadrilateral is a parallelogram if both pairs of opposite sides are parallel, both pairs of opposite sides are congruent, both pairs of opposite angles are congruent, consecutive angles are supplementary, one pair of opposite sides is congruent and parallel, or diagonals bisect each other. Figure B has both pairs of opposite sides congruent. Figure H has both pairs of opposite angles congruent. (See Student 1 in *Student Responses* section.) Some students choose B and H with incorrect reasoning. They see parallelograms as quadrilaterals with two congruent obtuse angles and two congruent acute angles. (See Student 2 in *Student Responses* section.)

- *Distracter A and D.* Although two right angles are given, there is not enough information to decide whether the other two angles are also right angles. In both figures the other angles appear to be right angles but are not necessarily. See figures on page 165 with same right angles as the ones in the probe. Many students see A as a rectangle and D as a square with opposite sides parallel. (See Students 3, 4, 5, 6, and 7 in *Student Responses* section.) This precision in the description of parallelograms usually appears at the Grades 9–12 level. In Grades 6 through 8, students generally consider A and D to be parallelograms as the specificity in labeling has not yet been explored.

- *Distracter C.* Students who choose this figure typically notice that there are several pairs of opposite parallel segments. Student overgeneralize the fact that parallelograms have to be quadrilateral with *both* sets of

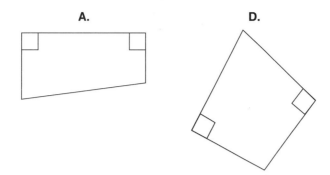

opposite sides parallel and think that if *all* sets of opposite sides are parallel it represents a parallelogram. (See Students 5 and 6 in *Student Responses* section.)

- *Distracter E.* This distracter is often picked by students who generally do not understand the properties of parallelograms. Some students have a *conceptual* misunderstanding of the opposite sides of this figure representing parallel lines. (See Students 6 and 7 in *Student Responses* section.)

- *Distracter F.* This distracter usually references a conceptual misunderstanding of the concepts of parallel lines and angles. The figure has no lines or angles, although some students will see this figure as having four line segments of the same length (and parallel) and four angles of same measure. (See Student 7 in *Student Responses* section.)

- *Distracter G.* Many students see the parallel line symbols and automatically relate the figure to parallelograms, not realizing that two sets of parallel sides are required. (See Students 6 and 7 in *Student Responses* section.)

Seeking Links to Cognitive Research

Students must carefully examine the features of shapes in order to precisely define and describe fundamental shapes, such as special types of quadrilaterals, and to identify relationships among the types of shapes. (NCTM, 2000, p. 233)

Although eighth-grade students believe that parallel lines should not intersect and should be equidistant, they also believe that parallel segments must be aligned and that curves might be parallel (Mansfield & Happs, 1992). (NCTM, 2003, p. 164)

Developing special sense . . . is a central goal of mathematics instruction that engenders problem solving in particular and doing mathematics in general. A strong special sense allows students to formulate image-based solutions to mathematics problems. Having a mental image of a parallelogram is fundamental. Without special sense, a student may only act mechanically with shapes and symbols that have little meaning. (NCTM, 2002, p. 148)

Teaching Implications

To support a deeper understanding for students in middle school in regard to parallelograms, the following are ideas and questions to consider in conjunction with the research.

Focus Through Instruction

- Students should explore a variety of geometric shapes and examine their characteristics.
- The use of materials such as geoboards, dot paper, multiple length cardboard strips with hinges, and dynamic geometry software to create two-dimensional shapes can be helpful
- multiple opportunities should be given to draw parallelograms of various shapes and sizes on a coordinate grid or with dynamic software
- Students should make and record measurements of the sides and angles of parallelograms to observe some of the characteristics properties
- Students should generate definitions for parallelograms that are correct and consistent with the commonly used ones and recognize the principal relationships among elements of parallelograms
- When students begin the use of specific labeling for parallelograms, care should be taken to accurately represent angles, congruency, and parallel lines
- Venn diagrams are useful in showing students all of the different types of quadrilaterals and certain properties that are shared among them

Questions to Consider . . . *when working with students as they grapple with the idea of parallelograms*

- Do students identify parallelograms given different geometric attributes?
- Do students apply the definition of a parallelogram to various shapes and sizes?
- Are students using accurate mathematical language to describe parallelograms?
- Do students recognize parallelograms as special quadrilaterals?
- Can students accurately recognize geometric labeling and symbols?

Teacher Sound Bite

"Unfortunately after I gave this probe to my students, I realized that I often draw figures similar to A and D. I am going to have to be very careful in the future to model accurate figures. We are going to have a class debate on all of these parallelograms to hopefully clear up some of the misunderstandings."

Additional References for Research and Teaching Implications

AAAS (1993), *Benchmarks for Science Literacy*, pp. 222–225, 352.

NCTM (1993a), *Research Ideas for the Classroom: Early Childhood Mathematics*, pp. 200–220.

NCTM (1993b), *Research Ideas for the Classroom: High School Mathematics*, pp. 140–147.

NCTM (1993c) *Research Ideas for the Classroom: Middle Grades Mathematics*, pp. 200–212.

NCTM (2000), *Principles and Standards for School Mathematics*, pp. 41–42, 97–98, 165–166, 233–234, 311.

NCTM (2002), *Reflecting on NCTM's Principles and Standards in Elementary and Middle School Mathematics*, pp. 147–158.

NCTM (2003), *Research Companion to Principles and Standards for School Mathematics*, pp. 151–156, 160, 164, 170.

> **Parallelograms**
>
> *Curriculum Topic Study*
>
> Related CTS Guide:
> Quadrilaterals

STUDENT RESPONSES TO "PARALLELOGRAMS"

Sample Response: BH (correct reasoning)

Student 1: B has two pairs of opposite sides that are parallel. H has two pairs of opposite angles that are congruent. A and D look like a rectangle and a square, but there is not enough information in the picture to be sure.

Sample Response: BH (incorrect reasoning)

Student 2: B and H are parallelograms because they both have four sides with two obtuse angles and two acute angles.

Sample Responses: Other Combinations

Student 3: I choose A, B, D, and H because they have parallel sides.

Student 4: A is a rectangle so it is also a parallelogram. I am not sure about B. It looks like a parallelogram, but it doesn't show the sides are parallel. D is a square and also a parallelogram. H also looks like a parallelogram.

Student 5: A, B, C, D, and H all have parallel sides so they are parallelograms.

Student 6: I think all of them but F are. All but F have at least one side parallel to another.

Student 7: C isn't a quadrilateral. All of the rest of these figures have parallel sides and must be parallelograms.

VOLUME OF A BOX

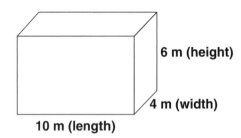

What is the volume of the box?

A. 20 m³

B. 240 m³

C. Not enough information

Explain your reasoning.

_____
_____
_____
_____

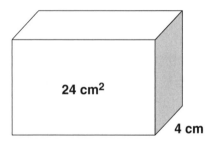

What is the volume of the box?

A. 28 cm³

B. 96 cm³

C. Not enough information

Explain your reasoning.

_____
_____
_____
_____

TEACHERS' NOTES: VOLUME OF A BOX

Grade Level for "Volume of a Box" Probe

Grades K–2	3–5	6–8	9–12
		███████	░░░░░░░

Questioning for Student Understanding

Do students understand how to find the volume of a box, given the side lengths or given the area of a face and the length of the other side?

Uncovering Understandings

Volume of a Box Content Standard: Measurement
Variation: Area of a Figure

Examining Student Work

The distracters may reveal students' lack of *procedural* understanding of the formula for volume or a lack of *conceptual* knowledge of area and volume.

- *The correct response for both boxes is B.* The volume of the first box is found by multiplying the length by the width by the depth (10m × 4m × 6m), which equals 20 m^3. For the second box, the area of one of the sides is given. To find the volume one needs to multiply the side area by the depth (24 cm^2 × 4cm), which equals 96 cm^3. (See Student 1 in *Student Responses* section.)
- *Distracter A.* Students typically choose this when they incorrectly add all of the side lengths together instead of multiplying. (See Student 2 in *Student Responses* section.)
- *Distracter C.* Most students may not choose C for the first box, but many do for the second. Students do not realize that by giving them the area of one of the sides, they already have the product of two of the side lengths and only need to multiply this by the third side length. Many students claim that they cannot find the volume unless the specific length of all of the sides is known. (See Students 3 and 4 in *Student Responses* section.)

Seeking Links to Cognitive Research

If students move rapidly to using formulas without an adequate conceptual foundation in area and volume, many students could have underlying confusions that would interfere with their working meaningfully with measurements. (NCTM, 2000, p. 242)

[There is] a distinction between understanding a formula numerically and understanding it quantitatively. (NCTM, 2003, p. 101)

*T*eaching Implications

To support a deeper understanding for students in middle school in regard to volume, the following are ideas and questions to consider in conjunction with the research.

Focus Through Instruction

- Concepts of area and volume should first be developed concretely, with procedures for computation following only when the concepts and some of their practical uses are well understood
- Students should have many informal experiences in understanding attributes of perimeter, area, and volume before using tools to measure them or relying on formulas to compute measurements
- The development of formulas of area and volume should be done by students through active engagement in hands-on experiences
- Students should make connections between the formula and an actual object
- Students should be given many opportunities to explore different area and volume problems and have discussions on different strategies to solve them
- Students should be able to communicate what information is given and in what form it appears

Questions to Consider . . . *when working with students as they grapple with the idea of volume*

- Do students have a conceptual understanding of volume, or do they rely on formulas?
- Can students communicate the information that is needed to find volume, and can they calculate it?
- Do students see the connection between volume and area?
- Have students developed strategies to determine volume of different shaped objects?

Teacher Sound Bite

"My students seem to understand how to find area and volume when given lengths of sides, but this probe has shown me that they lack conceptual knowledge of area and therefore volume."

Additional References for Research and Teaching Implications

AAAS (1993), *Benchmarks for Science Literacy,* pp. 222–225, 291, 293, 352.

NCTM (2000), *Principles and Standards for School Mathematics,* pp. 44–46, 171–175, 241–245.

NCTM (2003), *Research Companion to Principles and Standards for School Mathematics,* pp. 101–102, 181, 186–187.

Volume of a Box
Curriculum Topic Study
Related CTS Guide: Area and Volume

STUDENT RESPONSES TO "VOLUME OF A BOX"

Sample Response: B

Student 1: For the first box, you would multiply the length by the width by the height (10 × 6 × 4 = 240). For the second box, 24 is the area of the front face; therefore, it is the length × width. To get the volume, you would just need to multiply this by the height (24 × 4) to get 96.

Sample Response: A

Student 2: I chose A for both boxes because you add all the sides together to get the volume.

Sample Responses: C

Student 3: There is not enough information for the second box. You need the length of the box to get the volume.

Student 4: You need to have the height to find the volume in the second box.

VARIATION: AREA OF A FIGURE

What is the area of the rectangle?

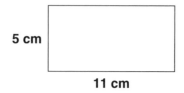

5 cm

11 cm

A. 32 cm²

B. 55 cm²

C. Not enough information

Explain your reasoning.

_____

_____

_____

_____

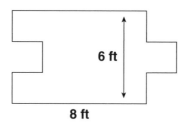

6 ft

8 ft

What is the area of the figure?

A. 48 ft²

B. 28 ft²

C. Not enough information

Explain your reasoning.

_____

_____

_____

_____

_____

_____

_____

Resource A

Note Template

___

Questioning for Student Understanding

___

Uncovering Understandings

___

Adaptations made to the probe:

___

Examining Student Thinking:

___

Seeking Links to Cognitive Research
Source:

___

Findings:

___

Source:

___

Findings:

___

Source:

_____

Findings:

_____

*T*eaching Implications

Source:

_____

Findings:

_____

Source:

_____

Findings:

_____

Source:

_____

Findings:

_____

Summary of Instructional Implications/Plan of Action:

_____

Results of Instruction:

_____

References

American Association for the Advancement of Science. (1993). *Benchmarks for science literacy.* New York: Oxford University Press.

Askew, M., & Wiliam, D. (1995). *Recent research in mathematics education 5–16.* London: HMSO Publications.

Bay Area Mathematics Task Force. (1999). *A mathematics source book for elementary and middle school teachers.* Novato, CA: Arena Press.

Borenson and Associates. (2005). *Hands-on equations.* Retrieved December 31, 2005, from http://www.borenson.com/html/whatis.html

Bright, G., & Joyner, J. (2004). *Dynamic classroom assessment: Linking mathematical understanding to instruction.* Vernon Hills, IL: ETA/Cuisenaire.

Burns, M. (2000). *About teaching mathematics: A K–8 resource.* Sausalito, CA: Math Solutions.

Burns, M. (2005). Looking at how students reason. *Educational Leadership: Assessment to Promote Learning, 63*(3), 26–31.

Clements, D., & Sarama, J. (2004). *Engaging young children in mathematics: Standards for early childhood mathematics education.* Mahwah, NJ: Lawrence Erlbaum.

Davies, A. (2000). *Making classroom assessment work.* British Columbia, Canada: Connections Publishing.

Dufour, R. (2001). Professional learning community. *The Leadership Academy Developer,* Missouri Department of Elementary & Secondary Education. Retrieved May 15, 2006, from http://info.csd.org/staffdev/rpdc/darticle.html

Fosnot, C., & Dolk, M. (2001). *Young mathematicians at work: Constructing number sense, addition, and subtraction.* Portsmouth, NH: Heinemann.

Griffin, P., & Madgwick, S. (2005). *Multiplication makes bigger and other mathematical myths.* Sowton, UK: DCS Publications.

Keeley, P., & Rose, C. (2006). *Mathematics curriculum topic study: Bridging the gap between standards and practice.* Thousand Oaks, CA: Corwin Press.

Leahy, S., Lyon, C., Thompson, M., & Wiliam, D. (2005). Classroom assessment: Minute by minute, day by day. *Educational Leadership: Assessment to Promote Learning, 63*(3), 19–24.

Lee, H.-J. (1999). *Resources for teaching and learning about probability and statistics* (ERIC Document No. ED433219). Retrieved December 27, 2005, from http://www.ericdigests.org/2000-2/resources.htm

Loucks-Horsley, S., Love, N., Stiles, K., Mundry, S., & Hewson, P. (2003). *Designing professional development for teachers of science and mathematics.* Thousand Oaks, CA: Corwin Press.

McTighe, J., & O'Conner, K. (2005). Seven practices for effective learning. *Educational Leadership: Assessment to Promote Learning, 63*(3), 10–17.

Mestre, J. (1987, Summer). Why should mathematics and science teachers be interested in cognitive research findings? *Academic Connections*, pp. 3–5, 8–11. New York: The College Board.

Mestre, J. (1989). Hispanic and Anglo students' misconceptions in mathematics (ERIC Document No. ED313192). *ERIC Digest*, Appalachia Educational Laboratory.

National Council of Teachers of Mathematics. (1993a). *Research ideas for the classroom: Early childhood mathematics.* New York: MacMillan.

National Council of Teachers of Mathematics. (1993b). *Research ideas for the classroom: High school mathematics.* New York: MacMillan.

National Council of Teachers of Mathematics. (1993c). *Research ideas for the classroom: Middle grades mathematics.* New York: MacMillan.

National Council of Teachers of Mathematics. (1999). *Algebraic thinking.* Reston, VA: Author.

National Council of Teachers of Mathematics. (2000). *Principles and standards for school mathematics.* Reston, VA: Author.

National Council of Teachers of Mathematics. (2001a). *Navigating through algebra in grades 6–8.* Reston, VA: Author.

National Council of Teachers of Mathematics. (2001b). *Navigating through algebra in grades 9–12.* Reston, VA: Author.

National Council of Teachers of Mathematics. (2002). *Reflecting on NCTM's Principles and Standards in Elementary and Middle School Mathematics.* Reston, VA: Author.

National Council of Teachers of Mathematics. (2003). *Research companion to principles and standards for school mathematics.* Reston, VA: Author.

National Council of Teachers of Mathematics. (2006a). *Teachers engaged in research: Inquiry into mathematics classrooms, grades 9–12.* Greenwich, CT: Information Age Publishing.

National Council of Teachers of Mathematics. (2006b). *Teachers engaged in research: Inquiry into mathematics classrooms, prekindergarten–grade2.* Greenwich, CT: Information Age Publishing.

National Research Council. (2001). *Adding it up: Helping children learn mathematics.* Washington, DC: National Academy Press

National Research Council. (2005). *How students learn: Mathematics in the classroom.* Washington, DC: National Academy Press

Naylor, S., & Keogh, B. (2000). *Concept cartoons in education.* Sandbach, UK: Millgate House.

Resnick, L. (1983). Mathematics and science learning: A new conception. *Science, 220,* 477–478.

Shaughnessy, M., & Ciancetta, M. (2002). *Students' understanding of the variability in a probability environment.* Retrieved May 14, 2006, from http://www.stat.auckland.ac.nz/~iase/publications/1/6a6_shau.pdf

Shell Centre for Mathematics Education & Joint Matriculaton Board. (1985). *The language of functions and graphs.* Nottingham, UK: Shell Centre for Mathematical Education.

Stavy, R., & Tirosh, D. (2000). *How students (mis-)understand science and mathematics.* New York: Teachers College Press.

Stepans, S., Schmidt, D., Welsh, K., Reins, K., & Saigo, B. (2005). *Teaching for K–12 mathematical understanding using the conceptual change model.* St. Cloud, MN: Saiwood.

Tomlinson, C. (1999). *The differentiated classroom: Meeting the needs of all learners.* Alexandria, VA: Association for Supervision and Curriculum Development.

University of Kansas. (2005). *Dynamic mathematics assessment.* Retrieved on December 31, 2005, from http://www.specialconnections.ku.edu/~specconn/page/instruction/math/pdf/patternanalysis.pdf

U.S. Department of Education, National Assessment Governing Board. (2003). *Mathematics framework for the 2003 National Assessment of Educational Progress.* Retrieved on December 31, 2005, from http://www.nagb.org/pubs/math_framework/ch4.html on 12/31/2005.

Van Dyke, F. (2002). *A visual approach to functions.* Emeryville, CA: Key Cuurriculum Press.

Wearne, D., & Hiebert, J. (2001). *Putting research into practice in the elementary grades: Reading from journals of the NCTM.* Reston, VA: National Council of Teachers of Mathematics.

Yetkin, E. (2003). *Student difficulties in learning elementary mathematics* (ERIC Document No. ED482727). Retrieved July 12, 2006, from http://www.ericdigests.org/2004-3/learning.html

Index

CORWIN PRESS

The Corwin Press logo—a raven striding across an open book—represents the union of courage and learning. Corwin Press is committed to improving education for all learners by publishing books and other professional development resources for those serving the field of PreK–12 education. By providing practical, hands-on materials, Corwin Press continues to carry out the promise of its motto: **"Helping Educators Do Their Work Better."**